TYNDALE
MOMENTUM®

A Tyndale nonfiction imprint

PRECIOUS IN HIS SIGHT

RACHEL NORMAN

A Mother's Guide to Praying for Her Children

Visit Tyndale online at tyndale.com.

Visit Tyndale Momentum online at tyndalemomentum.com.

Visit Rachel Norman at amotherfarfromhome.com.

Tyndale, Tyndale's quill logo, *Tyndale Momentum*, and the Tyndale Momentum logo are registered trademarks of Tyndale House Ministries. Tyndale Momentum is a nonfiction imprint of Tyndale House Publishers, Carol Stream, Illinois.

Precious in His Sight: A Mother's Guide to Praying for Her Children

Designed by Sarah Susan Richardson

Published in association with the literary agency of William K. Jensen Literary Agency, 119 Bampton Court, Eugene, Oregon 97404.

The prayers from *Little Folded Hands* by Louis Birk (St. Louis: Concordia Publishing House, 1912 ed.) and *Children's Prayers* by Sarah Wilson (London: Eyre & Spottiswoode, 1889) are in the public domain.

For information about special discounts for bulk purchases, please contact Tyndale House Publishers at csresponse@tyndale.com, or call 1-855-277-9400.

Library of Congress Cataloging-in-Publication Data

A catalog record for this book is available from the Library of Congress.

ISBN 978-1-4964-5984-8

Printed in China

30	29	28	27	26	25	24
7	6	5	4	3	2	1

For my precious ones:

Ella Kate, Judah, Fletch, Owie, and Hobby

Table of Contents

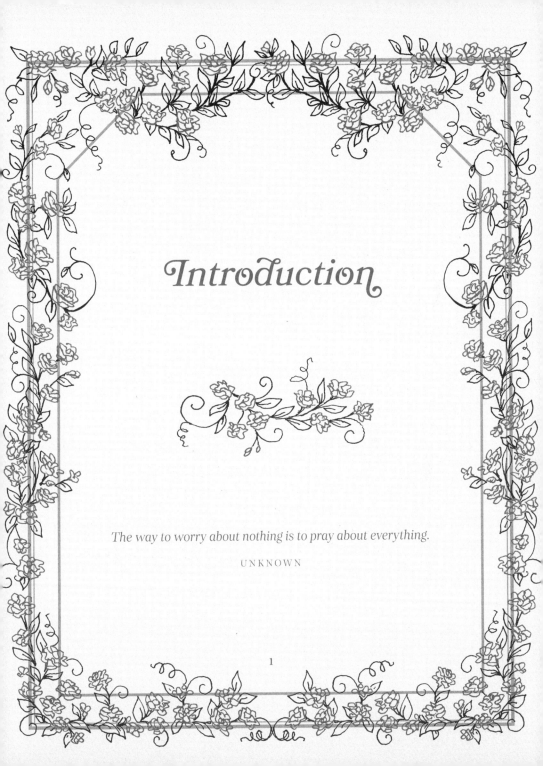

Introduction

The way to worry about nothing is to pray about everything.

UNKNOWN

THE AGONY AND THE ECSTASY.

That sums up motherhood.

We are overcome with delight, love, and affection for our little ones from the time they enter the world with their soft skin, baby smell, and toothless smiles. In that first year we're amazed by all they do, cheering our children's success with bodily functions and developmental milestones. We want everyone to treat them well and for life to be kind to them.

We agonize over whether they are happy, emotionally stable, and developing good character. We nitpick our parenting methods to be sure we are giving them the best shot at navigating what lies ahead. We protect them from harm and danger, worrying constantly about their environments and opportunities for mishap.

We are all in. And worn slam out.

I can remember lying in bed on countless nights feeling totally at the

end of my rope. It was my brain's favorite time to remind me of all my failures as a mother and how my kids were going to turn out bad if I didn't get it together—quickly.

I'd cycle through my feelings and usually end up arriving at the same place in my mind: *I can't be perfect, and I can't give my kids a perfect life.* But there was one thing—the best thing—I could give to my kids: fervent prayer.

You'd think that would have encouraged me. But alas, my inner critic doesn't give up that easily. As I was lying there, knowing I needed to pray more strategically and more often for my children, I just felt so . . . tired. Worn out. Uninspired. I wanted to lift my kids up to the Lord, but I just didn't have the words.

In fact, most of the times I prayed for my kids it was something like "God, help me!" While that is a perfectly valid and effective prayer, the call to deeper and more purposeful prayer lingered. If prayer is as important as Scripture says it is, then I needed to increase my use of this spiritual weapon in my life. God hears our prayers. Period.

What about you? Do you bring your children and their lives before Him regularly? Do you want to plant spiritual seeds and help water them until your child is walking closely with the Lord?

Of course, we all want to pray for our children! We're just bogged down with normal life and exhausted.

This book is designed to help overwhelmed, stressed, half-awake moms lift their children up to the Lord their God. No matter whether you're in a season of agony or ecstasy. When you aren't feeling creative, inspired, or led by God's Spirit, you can use this book to guide you in prayer for specific areas of your precious child's life.

One afternoon, as I was contemplating how to pray over my kids, I sat in my comfy chair with a hot drink in my Peter Rabbit teacup and opened my Bible to Psalm 66.

The first verse stood out to me:

Shout joyful praises to God, all the earth!

I continued reading the specific ways God had blessed His people in the past and in the present—more reasons for worshipful praise. And then I stopped again at verses 17 through 20.

I cried out to him for help, praising him as I spoke. If I had not confessed the sin in my heart, the Lord would not have listened. But God did listen! He paid attention to my prayer. Praise God, who did not ignore my prayer or withdraw his unfailing love from me.

We are to shout joyful praises to God, worshiping Him as we pray and call out for our children. And the last few verses of the psalm include an unexpected admission: The psalmist confessed he harbored sin in his heart that had become a barrier between him and God. I believe that act of repentance cleared his path to God. Like a staticky phone call, the connection was disrupted and communication with God was less clear. But after praising and repenting, the psalmist thanked God for hearing his prayers. Finally, he was able to release them, knowing the prayers were lovingly received.

As I reflected on the verses, an acronym came to mind that I've seen used over the years. I specifically adapted it to help me (and us!) pray over our precious ones.

(P) Praise God for something specific about your child.

(R) Repent for the ways you, like all the rest of us mamas, fall short from time to time.

(A) Ask God for whatever is on your heart for your child . . . something seemingly small or something so big you can hardly find the words for it.

(Y) Yield to His good purpose and plans for your child's life.

How to Use This Book

This book is not intended to be read from beginning to end—unless you want to! I've divided the book into the most pressing and important areas of our children's lives (their growth and development, health, talents and calling, school and education, salvation and spiritual growth, friendships, love and marriage, family life, and more). When you are ready to bring your child before the Lord, simply choose a section that speaks to your heart the most, or one that's most timely in your child's life.

Using the **PRAY** framework, you will be guided through a prayer time for your child, zeroing in on aspects of this particular area. I've created opening prayer suggestions, followed by a list of potential prayer prompt ideas to jump-start your requests. You don't have to use all of them—trust God to lead you.

Let's use the structure of "Salvation and Spiritual Growth" as an example. First, you'll see the instructional **PRAY** framework:

- **Praise.** Praise God that He calls us to Himself and has made a way for us in Jesus. If your child has surrendered their life to Jesus, you can praise God for that and rejoice for the times your child has listened to His Word.

- **Repent.** Ask the Lord to show you any areas in your family life where you've fallen short of what God wanted. Perhaps you didn't read your kids that devotion God put on your heart, or your schedule has gotten so busy you haven't taken them to church in several months. Repentance will reorient your heart toward God's will for your child.

- **Ask.** Open up and ask the Lord to grant your heart's desire for your child. You can use any of the prayer prompts provided in this section to help you. You might request that your child would have discernment, spiritual hunger, love for God's Word, or anything else God brings to mind. In addition, there are Bible verses that relate directly to the topic so you can pray Scripture over your child.

- **Yield.** After praying through your desires for your precious child, take a minute and surrender those prayers, thoughts, and emotions to your heavenly Father. Leave them with Him, knowing He cares for you and your child.

Then you'll see the series of specific prayer prompts:

ℒord, I pray my child shows . . .

> a *readiness* to follow God's will
> strong *moral character*
> *delight in serving* others

The Scripture verses that come next can be read, recited as prayers, or even memorized as a family:

> Create in me a clean heart, O God.
>   Renew a loyal spirit within me.
> PSALM 51:10

The verses are followed by short prayers you can use as written or personalize:

𝒜 foundation of strong biblical teaching.

> Heavenly Father, I am thankful for the church and for teachers who love You and explain Your love to my child. May the lessons they share from Your Word take root in my child's heart.

And finally, the section closes with a blessing:

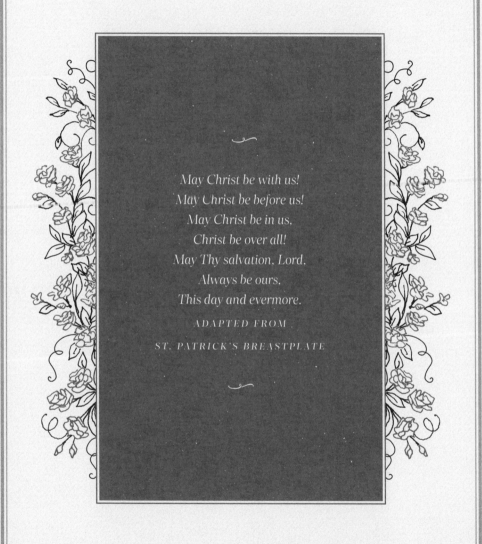

May Christ be with us!
May Christ be before us!
May Christ be in us,
Christ be over all!
May Thy salvation, Lord,
Always be ours,
This day and evermore.

ADAPTED FROM
ST. PATRICK'S BREASTPLATE

Each section of this book will end with a selection of written prayers, Scripture to pray over your child, and a closing blessing. My prayer is that as you bring your requests before God and dive into His Word, you will be refreshed and grow in faith. The more you use this book, the more insights God will give you on how to intercede for your child. All He wants you to do is show up.

As A. W. Tozer wisely said, "The key to prayer is simply praying."

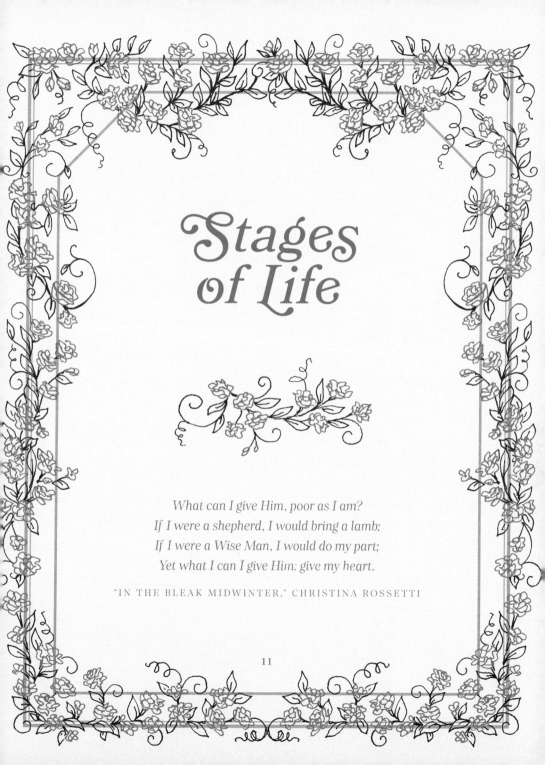

Stages
of Life

What can I give Him, poor as I am?
If I were a shepherd, I would bring a lamb;
If I were a Wise Man, I would do my part;
Yet what I can I give Him: give my heart.

"IN THE BLEAK MIDWINTER," CHRISTINA ROSSETTI

MOTHERS HAVE THE PRIVILEGE of watching their little one grow up. Sometimes it feels like overnight! The hard times seem to last forever, and the sweet times seem to fly by. One of the best ways to take advantage of these precious moments with your child, and not take them for granted, is to surrender to every life season.

In the early years, I surrendered to cocooning a lot at home and living at a slower pace. At times, I felt I'd withdrawn from life and, in a way, I had. I'd withdrawn from a busier social life to focus on my family. As my children became more active, I surrendered to their questions and curiosities. (They have lots of questions and repeat them often!) Now, as they become more and more independent, I surrender to long conversations and lessening the controls to help them learn to fly.

During every stage of their life, bathe your precious child in prayer.

raise. Thank the Lord for the privilege of being a mother. Let the memories or blessings come to your mind and offer up a gift of praise and thanksgiving to God, who has given you a child to raise here on earth. It is an enormous privilege. Motherhood is one of your many roles and a primary purpose that God created you for. Thank the Lord for this!

epent. If you've lived in fear or gone off the narrow path, share the details with the Lord with a contrite heart. Have you rebelled against Him or strayed from the truths in His Word? He will kindly lead you toward genuine repentance and change. Be renewed in your mind by the Holy Spirit as He realigns your priorities.

sk. Ask the Lord to bring to mind anything you need to pray about. Using the prayer prompts and Scripture verses, ask the Lord to remember His promises to His people. Lift up your child's needs at every stage of their life and believe the Lord of lords and King of kings cares about your precious child more than you do.

ield. After a time of praise and prayer, surrender these dreams, hopes, requests, and fears to the Lord. If you're a visual person, imagine putting your prayers on the altar (or some other safe significant place) and leaving them there for God to deal with in His time.

Lord Jesus, I'm pregnant and ask for . . .

    healthy development of the baby
    peace and safety for the child within my womb
    calmness for me
    a *smooth pregnancy* without complications at any point
    a *caring* and attentive *birth team*
    a *safe labor* and delivery
    a *non-traumatic birth*

Lord, I pray my young child will have . . .

    on-track *developmental milestones*
    curiosity and creativity in play
    protection from accidents
    security and safety at home
    a strong *sense of right and wrong*
    comfort for fears and anxieties
    exposure to *biblical teaching*
    remorse when they disobey
    no terrible twos, threes, or fearsome fours
    a *strong immune system*
    secure attachment to caregivers

Lord, I pray my preteen and teenager will have . . .

a strong *relationship with* their *parent(s)*
open lines of *communication*
freedom to explore interests
an *appreciation* for parental input
a *godly* group of faithful *friends*
a *desire to* discover and *utilize gifts* and passions
an ability to live within *convictions*
growth in their relationship *with God*
security in how God created them
acceptance of the *schooling decisions*
focus and *diligence in* their *schoolwork*

Lord, I pray my maturing young adult will have . . .

a *strong work ethic*
a *clear sense of* their true job and *calling*
the gift of *a godly spouse*
an *aversion to* besetting *sins*
a *positive* and enthusiastic *outlook* on life
a *foundation of faith* from their youth
opportunities to serve others
healthy friendships
direction from God in major life choices
confidence and security in their abilities

*L*ord, I pray my middle-aged child will have . . .

a firm sense of *purpose*
fulfilling and godly *relationships*
success in their chosen career or calling
an *active* and fulfilling *social life*
opportunities to minister and serve God
a *vision* for the next phase of life
an impactful *relationship with children* and grandchildren
secure and *stable housing*

Pray through these verses.

Before I formed you in the womb I knew you, before you were born I set you apart; I appointed you as a prophet to the nations.

JEREMIAH 1:5, NIV

You shall love the LORD your God with all your heart and with all your soul and with all your might. And these words that I command you today shall be on your heart. You shall teach them diligently to your children, and shall talk of them when you sit in your house, and when you walk by the way, and when you lie down, and when you rise.

DEUTERONOMY 6:5-7, ESV

Wisdom belongs to the aged,
and understanding to the old.

JOB 12:12

The glory of the young is their
strength;
the gray hair of experience is the
splendor of the old.

PROVERBS 20:29

Sample Prayer ───────

God, You formed [child's name] in my womb and gave them specific qualities, talents, and gifts to glorify You. Please guide my child throughout their life to the right path that honors You. Amen.

_____

_____

_____

_____

_____

_____

_____

_____

_____

_____

_____

_____

You brought me safely from my
    mother's womb
  and led me to trust you at my
    mother's breast.
I was thrust into your arms at my
    birth.
  You have been my God from the
    moment I was born.

PSALM 22:9-10

Now that I am old and my hair is
    gray, don't leave me, God.
  I must tell the next generation
    about your power and
    greatness.
God, your goodness reaches far above
    the skies.
  You have done wonderful things.
  God, there is no one like you.

PSALM 71:18-19, ERV

For you created my inmost being;
  you knit me together in my
    mother's womb.
I praise you because I am fearfully and
    wonderfully made;
  your works are wonderful,
  I know that full well.
My frame was not hidden from you
  when I was made in the secret
    place,
  when I was woven together in the
    depths of the earth.

Your eyes saw my unformed body;
    all the days ordained for me were
        written in your book
    before one of them came to be.

PSALM 139:13-16, NIV

Train up a child in the way he
    should go;
    even when he is old he will not
        depart from it.

PROVERBS 22:6, ESV

One day some parents brought their children to Jesus so he could touch and bless them. But the disciples scolded the parents for bothering him.

When Jesus saw what was happening, he was angry with his disciples. He said to them, "Let the children come to me. Don't stop them! For the Kingdom of God belongs to those who are like these children. I tell you the truth, anyone who doesn't receive the Kingdom of God like a child will never enter it." Then he took the children in his arms and placed his hands on their heads and blessed them.

MARK 10:13-16

Personalize these prayers.

Safe labor and delivery.

Lord Jesus, I pray that I will have a safe labor and delivery of my child. May I be able to relax, stay calm, and trust the birth team around me to bring my precious baby into the world without incident or complication. Help me to trust the natural process You set in motion, Lord. In Jesus' name, amen.

Protection from accidents.

I praise You, Lord, that children learn and grow through play. I pray that as my child's curiosity grows and they seek out new experiences in life, they are protected from accidents or mishaps that could cause physical harm. Thank you, Lord. Amen.

Strong relationship with parents.

I pray that I will have a close relationship with my child throughout their life. Whenever there are misunderstandings or estrangement, help us repent, forgive, repair, and restore our relationship. May the closeness between us be a source of strength for us all in years to come.

Listens and values parental input.

As my child approaches adolescence, their teen years, and young adulthood, please help us to have the type of relationship where they come to me for answers to questions and value my input. Help me to understand their perspective, give me wisdom for each stage of their life, and please prevent anything from becoming an obstacle between us.

Curiosity and creativity in play.

Please help my child be creative, curious, and interested in life, instead of becoming isolated or too shy to join in. I pray you protect them from perfectionism, insecurity, or anything that would cause them to shut down and not engage fully in activities and everyday living.

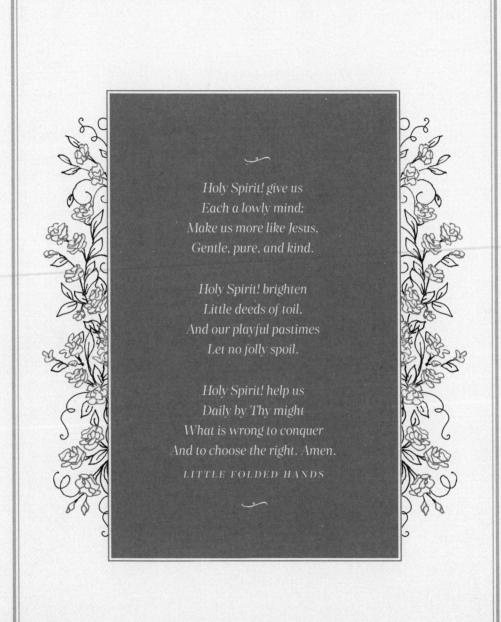

Holy Spirit! give us
Each a lowly mind;
Make us more like Jesus,
Gentle, pure, and kind.

Holy Spirit! brighten
Little deeds of toil,
And our playful pastimes
Let no folly spoil.

Holy Spirit! help us
Daily by Thy might
What is wrong to conquer
And to choose the right. Amen.

LITTLE FOLDED HANDS

Sons

The man who has God for his treasure has all things in One.

A. W. TOZER

25

As a mother of four boys (all born within four years), I have experienced the gamut of little-boy energy. The wild abandon of aggressive play, the sweet quiet cuddles, and everything in between. Being a mother is one of the greatest privileges and joys a woman can have, and it brings with it so much emotion, doesn't it?

Let's use those feelings and emotions to draw us near to our Lord in prayer for our precious sons.

Praise. Was your son long awaited? A pleasant surprise? Praise God for how He's made your son—for his personality, his talents and gifts—and for all of God's plans for your son. Really lift him up to the Lord with thanksgiving and praise in your heart. Take this time to show gratitude to the Lord for all the ways He's blessed your son up to this point.

Repent. Allow the Holy Spirit to pinpoint anything you need to address before the Lord. Are there overwhelming fears or worries that control you regarding your son? Have you made choices you haven't taken to the cross yet? Or have you neglected to do things you know the Lord required of you? Take time in this still and quiet moment to talk them over with Jesus.

Ask. Using the given prayer prompts or your own requests inspired by the Holy Spirit, confidently bring your requests to the Lord. The Word says He hears us when we ask according to His will. Pray Scripture and express your heart's desires for your son and for God's will to be done in his life. Don't rush—allow time for your heart to really connect with the Lord.

Yield. After having presented your requests before the Lord, surrender them to Him. We cannot control much of what happens in this world, and that alone can lead to worry and anxiety. Even though you won't be there in every moment of your son's life, release him to the Lord, who will be there. He will never leave or forsake your son.

Lord, I pray my son will have . . .

an *opportunity to accept Jesus* at a young age
courage in adversity
a *tender heart* toward God
discernment of good and evil
strong *resistance to temptation*
faithfulness in relationships
Christlike love for his future family
speedy *repentance*
honesty in his words and deeds
times to be fair and just in his dealings
godly *lasting friendships*
good old-fashioned *common sense*
physical and mental *strength*
leadership qualities
regular *communion with God*
Scripture meditation practices
protection from selfish ambition
a goal of *excellence*, not perfectionism
an *aversion to* besetting *sins*
wise mentors and advisors
strength to resist the devil
a *sober mind* and alertness
freedom from lust
a *grateful heart*

healthy *self-confidence*
identity in Christ
a *teachable* heart
a *humble spirit*
a *spiritual vision* to see how God is working
a *passion* for things of God
a *heart to hear* God's voice
obedience to God's Word
consistent stewardship of resources
no struggles with *depression*
emotional freedom before God
a *healthy sense of self*
an *eagerness to be generous* with talents and time
loyalty to friends and as a future husband
a *strong work ethic*
no participation in *foolish behavior*
a clear sense of *purpose*
Christlike love for family
no stronghold of *fear*
an *eternal perspective* in life
protection from secret sin
wisdom and *integrity in financial matters*
a keen sense of *justice*
understanding and slowness to anger with those he loves

Pray through these verses.

"In the last days," God says,
    "I will pour out my Spirit upon all
        people.
Your sons and daughters will prophesy.
    Your young men will see visions,
    and your old men will dream
        dreams.
In those days I will pour out my Spirit
    even on my servants—men and
        women alike—
    and they will prophesy."

ACTS 2:17-18

Have I not commanded you? Be
strong and courageous. Do not be
afraid; do not be discouraged, for
the LORD your God will be with
you wherever you go.

JOSHUA 1:9, NIV

Blessed is the one
    who does not walk in step with
        the wicked
or stand in the way that sinners take
    or sit in the company of mockers,
but whose delight is in the law of
        the LORD,
    and who meditates on his law day
    and night.

Sample Prayer

*God, Your Word says You'll pour
out Your Spirit on all people and
that your sons and daughters
will speak for You. I pray that
[child's name] will have visions,
dreams, and revelation from Your
Word to be strengthened and to
strengthen others.*

That person is like a tree planted by
    streams of water,
    which yields its fruit in season
and whose leaf does not wither—
    whatever they do prospers.

PSALM 1:1-3, NIV

The LORD is with me; I will not be
    afraid.
    What can mere mortals do to me?

PSALM 118:6, NIV

How can a young person stay on the
    path of purity?
    By living according to your word.
I seek you with all my heart;
    do not let me stray from your
    commands.
I have hidden your word in my heart
    that I might not sin against you.

PSALM 119:9-11, NIV

If you think you are standing
strong, be careful not to fall.
The temptations in your life are
no different from what others
experience. And God is faithful.
He will not allow the temptation
to be more than you can stand.
When you are tempted, he will
show you a way out so that you
can endure.

1 CORINTHIANS 10:12-13

Be on guard. Stand firm in the faith.
Be courageous. Be strong.

1 CORINTHIANS 16:13

But you, man of God, flee from
all this, and pursue righteousness,
godliness, faith, love, endurance and
gentleness. Fight the good fight of
the faith. Take hold of the eternal
life to which you were called when
you made your good confession in
the presence of many witnesses.

1 TIMOTHY 6:11-12, NIV

You who are younger must accept
the authority of the elders. And all
of you, dress yourselves in humility
as you relate to one another, for
"God opposes the proud
but gives grace to the humble."

1 PETER 5:5

Be alert and of sober mind. Your
enemy the devil prowls around like a
roaring lion looking for someone to
devour. Resist him, standing firm in
the faith, because you know that the
family of believers throughout the
world is undergoing the same kind
of sufferings.

1 PETER 5:8-9, NIV

Personalize these prayers.

Quick to repent.

Dear Lord, I pray [child's name] would have a heart that's teachable and sensitive to the Holy Spirit. I'm asking You to convict him when necessary and that his heart would be quick to repent, quick to turn to You, and quick to change course. Help my son walk in the Spirit all his days. In Jesus' name, amen.

Courage in adversity.

Dear Jesus, please give [child's name] courage in the face of adversity. When life gets hard and challenges mount up, the path isn't clear, or he knows doing the right thing might cause more problems, I pray my son would have supernatural fortitude from You. Amen.

Freedom from lust.

God, I pray [child's name] would fight the lust that is so prevalent in our culture. Keep his heart pure and give him courage to strongly resist the fleshly desires that could lead him away from You. Help my son to remain faithful to Your Word. Amen.

Good old-fashioned common sense.

Lord Jesus, I pray [child's name] would have common sense, wisdom, and good judgment to make the right decisions. Prevent my son from outsmarting his common sense or making decisions that will come back to bite him later. In Jesus' name, amen.

Honesty in word and deed.

Please convict [child's name] to always be a person who exhibits honesty and integrity. May he act, think, and operate with a desire for life-giving truth. I pray my son will be a trustworthy and honorable man of God. In Jesus' name, amen.

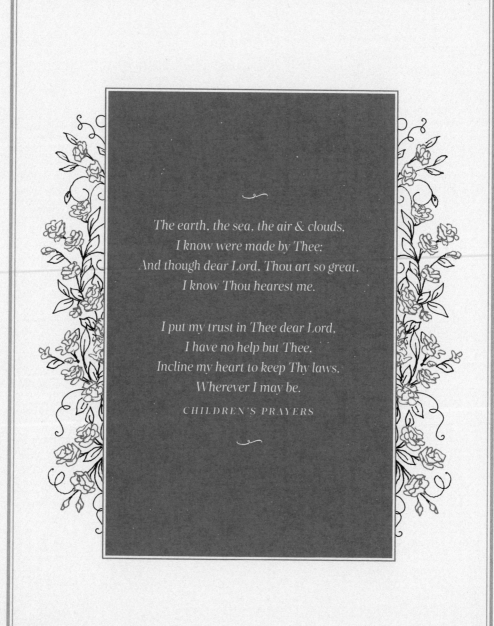

The earth, the sea, the air & clouds,
I know were made by Thee;
And though dear Lord, Thou art so great,
I know Thou hearest me.

I put my trust in Thee dear Lord,
I have no help but Thee.
Incline my heart to keep Thy laws,
Wherever I may be.

CHILDREN'S PRAYERS

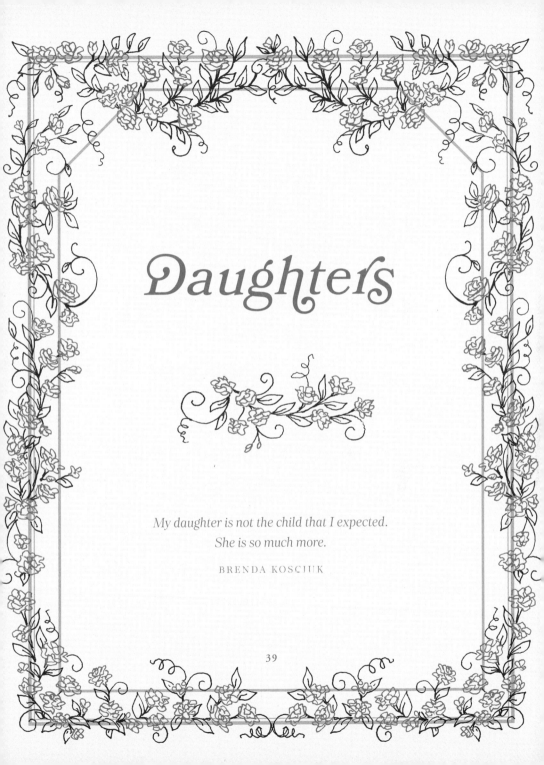

Daughters

My daughter is not the child that I expected.
She is so much more.

BRENDA KOSCIUK

I REMEMBER WHEN my daughter was born on a sunny day in Scotland. My labor was quick, and as I held her in my arms for the first time, my husband and I looked out the window and saw a large, beautiful rainbow. We were amazed at the display, a reminder of God's promises (Genesis 9).

From the beginning, I was fascinated by all my daughter did, and my wonder continued throughout her early years of childhood. It's a privilege and honor to help nurture her heart and soul as she begins her journey into womanhood. I pray you can lift your daughter up to the Lord in a way that creates a strong bond that lasts a lifetime and into eternity.

Praise. Begin by praising God for fearfully and wonderfully creating your daughter (see Psalm 139:14, NIV). Thank Him for how He's cared for her and how He loves her more than even you can. Spend some time lifting up your daughter to the Lord.

Repent. Ask the Lord if there's any area relating to your daughter where you need to repent, forgive, or change course. Without feeling guilty or self-condemning, allow the Lord to highlight any areas that need addressing. Meditate on anything God reveals to you.

Ask. Scripture instructs us to come boldly to the throne to make our requests to God (see Hebrews 4:16). Using the prayer prompts given or any others that spring to mind, lift up your daughter to the Lord and ask Him to care for her and draw her near to Himself. Ask that He would go before her and make her way straight throughout her life.

Yield. After bringing your requests to God, give your concerns and fears for your daughter to the Lord. Releasing our children to the Lord feels like we're losing something. But truthfully, we don't have control over our children's lives, and the sooner we're able to surrender their futures to Him, the more peace we'll feel.

Lord, I pray my daughter will have . . .

identity as a daughter of the King
security in God
deep *abiding friendships*
healthy *acceptance of changes* in her body
comfort with femininity
no confusion around identity
self-control
guidance from God throughout life
peace and *assurance* during trying times
conviction of the Holy Spirit
values found in God
unwavering convictions
many healthy *outlets for stress relief*
a *steadfast spirit*
protection from accidents
a *desire for God's approval*, not the world's
courage to stand up for herself
godly mentors, teachers, and coaches
future friends, roommates, and *coworkers who love God*
a *future spouse* (if that's God's will)
godly standards
a *hunger for God's Word*
a *heart to love and serve* others
a *yearning* to follow God's will
spiritual discernment

a *shield* from deception
clarity regarding gifts and callings
excellent physical *health*
a *grateful* and appreciative *heart*
mental and emotional health
an *ability* to recognize the Lord's voice
no attraction to the world's beauty standards
keen intuition and reliable instincts
self-discipline in important matters
protection from abusers
beautiful character and personality
revelation of secret dangers or *sins*
a *sharp mind*, soft heart, and thick skin
God's power to break curses or thwart evil plans against her
freedom from generational sin or *trauma*
eloquence in sharing her faith
an *ability to resist the devil* and stand firm against temptation
wisdom in online activity
care for her physical body
regular and *persistent prayer*
fitting career choices
a *lifelong walk with the Spirit*, not the flesh
warnings and prophecies *that help direct her* paths
a strong and healthy *connection with family* members
an abiding *relationship with God*

Pray through these verses.

Charm is deceptive, and beauty does
    not last;
    but a woman who fears the LORD
      will be greatly praised.

PROVERBS 31:30

The LORD is my strength and shield.
    I trust him with all my heart.
He helps me, and my heart is filled
      with joy.
    I burst out in songs of
      thanksgiving.

PSALM 28:7

Thank you for making me so
      wonderfully complex!
    Your workmanship is marvelous—
      how well I know it.

PSALM 139:14

A wise woman builds her home,
    but a foolish woman tears it down
      with her own hands.

PROVERBS 14:1

Sample Prayer

*God, I pray that [child's name]
will fear you, praise you, and value
godliness over natural beauty.
In Jesus' name, amen.*

_____

_____

_____

_____

_____

_____

_____

_____

_____

_____

_____

_____

She goes to inspect a field and buys it;
with her earnings she plants a
vineyard.

PROVERBS 31:16

She is energetic and strong,
a hard worker.

PROVERBS 31:17

Strength and dignity are her clothing,
and she laughs at the time to
come.

PROVERBS 31:25, ESV

When she speaks, her words are wise,
and she gives instructions with
kindness.

PROVERBS 31:26

My lover said to me,
"Rise up, my darling!
Come away with me, my fair one!"

SONG OF SONGS 2:10

You are blessed because you
believed that the Lord would do
what he said.

LUKE 1:45

Personalize these prayers.

Identity as a daughter of the King.

Lord God, I pray [child's name] would have a deep
abiding relationship with You. I ask that she will discuss
her hopes, dreams, problems, anxieties, and anything
in between with You. May Your constant presence be a
rock-solid reality in my daughter's life and her source of
hope and security. Amen.

Finds her value in God.

Dear Jesus, help [child's name]'s heart become more
and more like Yours so she is less tempted by things
of the world (James 1:14). When my daughter faces
temptation, I pray she would hold firmly to Your Word
and resist the enemy. In Your precious name, amen.

Strong convictions.

Dear Lord, let the truth of Your Word permeate
all [child's name]'s being and help protect her from
deception found in empty philosophies, promoted
by the culture around her, or resulting from painful
circumstances that may happen to her. Please put
people in my daughter's life who will speak truth to
her spirit. Amen.

Courage to stand up for herself.

Dear Jesus, I pray you'd give [child's name] courage to stand up for herself and others when needed. Help my daughter feel confident and sure when she needs to speak up about an injustice or correct a wrong. Protect her from being bullied, abused, or mistreated. Let her claim her incalculable worth as a daughter of the Most High. Amen.

Comfort with femininity.

Lord God, I pray you'd help [child's name] feel comfortable in her own skin. As my daughter's body changes and matures and she becomes a young lady, then a young woman, then a mature woman, I pray she is comfortable and proud of how You made her. Help her know she is a temple of the Holy Spirit and well loved by You. In Jesus' name, amen.

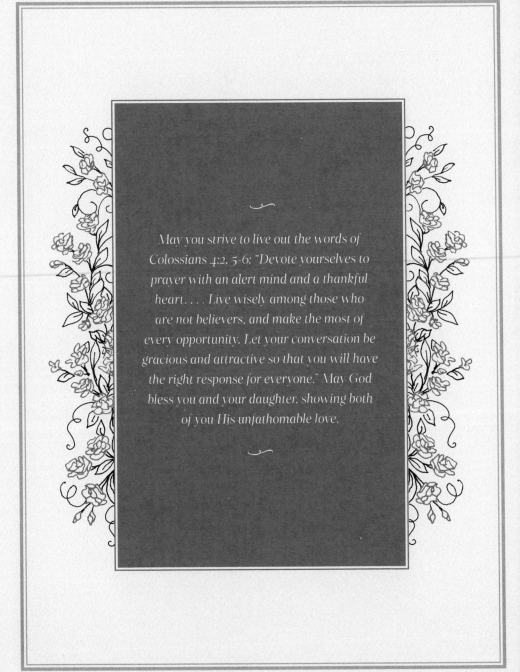

May you strive to live out the words of Colossians 4:2, 5-6: "Devote yourselves to prayer with an alert mind and a thankful heart. . . . Live wisely among those who are not believers, and make the most of every opportunity. Let your conversation be gracious and attractive so that you will have the right response for everyone." May God bless you and your daughter, showing both of you His unfathomable love.

Health

Tender Jesus, meek and mild,
Look on me, a little child;
Help me, if it is Thy will,
To recover from all ill. Amen.

LITTLE FOLDED HANDS

Let's be honest. Many parents' fears center around their child's health and well-being. We know that safety on this earth is not guaranteed, but we are desperate to keep our little one safe and protected.

When our child is an infant, we babyproof their surroundings and are hypervigilant as they age. Our nervous systems and internal danger monitors are attuned to their every move. As they get older, we loosen the reins in some ways, but our minds begin to spin with all the additional possibilities of things that could go wrong.

We love our precious one so much that we want them to have an easy road ahead—clear, straightforward paths with few obstacles or steep summits to climb. Unfortunately, we cannot make their crooked paths smooth and straight or level the mountains they encounter.

But thanks be to God—He can!

Let's come to the Lord in prayer, lifting up our dear child's health—from infancy to maturity—knowing that we can only do so much. The rest is out of our control.

Praise. Lift your precious one up to the Lord, praising Him for how He fearfully and wonderfully formed your child. Thank God for any specific situations that come to mind where God's provision or timely intervention resulted in continued health for your child.

Repent. With a tender heart, ask the Lord to reveal any area that needs realigning with His Word. Are you overly anxious about your child's emotional, mental, or physical health? Do you need to cast those cares on God without taking them back to stew on? Go before the Lord without self-condemnation or shame and ask Him to reveal anything you need to revisit or recalibrate.

Ask. Bring your heart's desires for your child to the Lord. Use the prayer prompts that follow or anything the Holy Spirit brings to mind. Pray Scripture over your child and ask the Lord to watch over your child's health now and forever. Pray through your worries, fears, and anxieties.

Yield. After you've presented your requests to the Lord, it's time to yield them to Him. Surrender is, of course, one of the hardest parts of our spiritual walk with the Lord, but it's also one of the most freeing. As a mother, you do all you can, and then you must release the burden to the Lord, knowing He hears our requests.

Dear Lord, thank you for making us emotional human beings. Give my child . . .

a *forgiving heart*
freedom from grudges
an *openness* to express feelings
a *willingness* to confess sins
healthy conversations with friends and family
courage to face painful situations
persistence to wrestle with God about doubts
joy in Jesus
clean and *positive times* of fun
readiness to express emotions
no stronghold of *fear*
a *happy attitude* and heart
self-control from an explosive temper
compassion for those in need
no tendency toward *self-pity*
an *encouraging heart* for others
fearlessness, not fearfulness
a *tranquil heart*
age-appropriate *emotional maturity*

Dear Lord, thank You for creating us with complex brains and equipping us to think about the world and our purpose in it. Give my child . . .

freedom from perfectionism
protection from intrusive thoughts
resilience during stressful times
a *sound mind*
realistic levels of *self-control*
strength and *courage to stand up* for values
assertive communication
humility and wisdom
peace of mind in all situations
a *shield* against temptation
opportunity (if needed) *to wrestle with God* without cynicism
an *appreciation* for wise counsel
true friends and escape from loneliness
an *acceptance* of temporary suffering
courage to make necessary changes
resistance to bitterness and resentment
a *renewed mind*
steadfast trust in Jesus
a *focus on noble* and good *things*
a *Spirit-influenced mindset*
singleness of mind and purpose

Jesus, I am thankful that we are wonderfully made and have physical bodies to honor and glorify You. Give my child . . .

a *healthy immune system*
strong bones
on-track development
protection from accidents
acceptance of their body type and figure
discipline and healthy habits
awareness of their body's needs
an *understanding* that their body is God's temple
courage to bring up health issues
intuitive health care providers
pragmatism to not take needless risks
balanced hormones
good vision
revelation of hidden *physical issues*
resilience from common ailments
peace regarding medical interventions
freedom from making fitness or perfection an idol

Pray through these verses.

Don't you realize that your body is the temple of the Holy Spirit, who lives in you and was given to you by God? You do not belong to yourself, for God bought you with a high price. So you must honor God with your body.

1 CORINTHIANS 6:19-20

You must serve only the LORD your God. If you do, I will bless you with food and water, and I will protect you from illness.

EXODUS 23:25

He heals the brokenhearted
    and bandages their wounds.

PSALM 147:3

Don't be impressed with your own
        wisdom.
    Instead, fear the LORD and turn
        away from evil.
Then you will have healing for your
        body
    and strength for your bones.

PROVERBS 3:7-8

Sample Prayer

God, I lift up [child's name]'s body to you right now and pray that it would be a sacred place. Please help [name] to honor you with their body and choices.

A cheerful heart is good medicine,
　　but a broken spirit saps a person's
　　　strength.

PROVERBS 17:22

Refuse to worry, and keep your
body healthy.

ECCLESIASTES 11:10

For you who fear my name, the
Sun of Righteousness will rise
with healing in his wings. And
you will go free, leaping with joy
like calves let out to pasture.

MALACHI 4:2

He personally carried our sins
　　in his body on the cross
so that we can be dead to sin
　　and live for what is right.
By his wounds
　　you are healed.

1 PETER 2:24

I hope all is well with you and
that you are as healthy in body
as you are strong in spirit.

3 JOHN 1:2

Personalize these prayers.

Doesn't hold grudges.

> Lord Jesus, I pray [child's name] would not let anger grow into grudges against someone else. I pray that when feelings are hurt and pain sets in, my child could learn to forgive so they aren't bound by bitter roots of judgment. In Jesus' name, amen.

Acceptance of body type and figure.

> Dear Lord, I pray [child's name] will embrace the body You gave them. May they be healthy inside and out and not compare themselves to others and rob themselves of joy. Amen.

Healthy openness with friends and family.

> May [child's name] be open and willing to interact with their friends and family instead of being too private to really be known. I pray You'd guide me to emotionally support and love my child in the way they need.

Freedom from perfectionism.

> Heavenly Father, protect [child's name] from the ball
> and chain of perfectionism. I know the adverse effect
> perfectionism can have on people, causing them to panic
> from the pressure and making them feel everything they
> do isn't quite good enough. Lord, remove any yoke of
> perfectionism from my precious child so they can achieve
> the purpose You have for them. In Your Son's name,
> amen.

Finds joy in Jesus.

> Dear Jesus, I pray [child's name] would recognize Your
> presence and build a life that is welcoming and hospitable
> to the Holy Spirit. May the joy of the Lord truly be the
> strength of my child in any hard days to come. Amen.

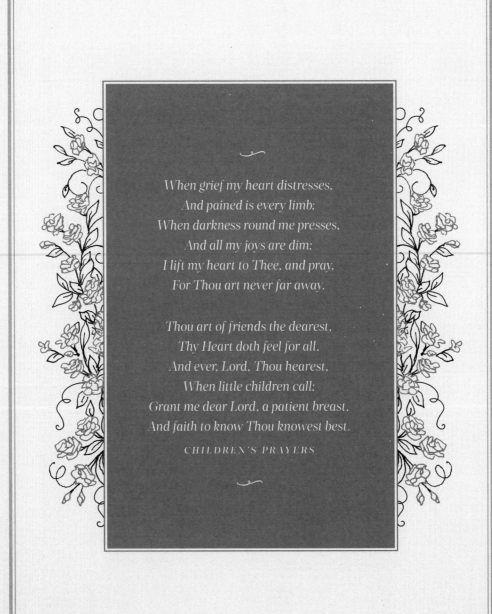

When grief my heart distresses,
And pained is every limb:
When darkness round me presses,
And all my joys are dim:
I lift my heart to Thee, and pray,
For Thou art never far away.

Thou art of friends the dearest,
Thy Heart doth feel for all.
And ever, Lord, Thou hearest,
When little children call:
Grant me dear Lord, a patient breast.
And faith to know Thou knowest best.

CHILDREN'S PRAYERS

Talents, Interests, Callings & Careers

On what has now been sown
Thy blessing, Lord, bestow;
The power is Thine alone
To make it spring and grow. Amen.

LITTLE FOLDED HANDS

❧ I OFTEN DREAM ABOUT what my children will do with their lives once they've spread their wings and flown the coop. Will they live nearby or far away? Will they work with their hands, create something on a computer, or excel in a career not yet imagined? I help them try new things and dig deeper into their interests, hoping they can discover what talents and gifts God has given them to be used for His glory.

Whether your child uses their spiritual gifts, talents, and interests to forge a career, or they use them exclusively in the church or as side hobbies, let's make sure to bathe these things in prayer. Allow God to guide and direct your child to the paths they should take at the right times throughout their lives.

Praise. Thank the Lord for giving your child the gifts He has chosen for them. Acknowledge the various talents or strengths your child has and let God know how proud and grateful you are for these unique characteristics He has given them. Praise Him for the way He will guide, lead, and use your child's personality, gifts, and talents to bless others throughout their life.

Repent. Humbly go before the Lord and let Him reveal anything in your life that needs to be confessed. Has the Lord asked you to do something you've refused? Have you let fear get in the way of living out your own calling or career? Do you see God's hand in your own life at various times, leading you this way or that, and you were too busy to stop and respond? Take it to God!

Ask. Using whatever words the Holy Spirit gives you, petition the Lord to show up mightily for your child throughout their life. Ask Him to reveal your child's passions and talents at an age where they can learn to steward them well. Pray through the provided prompts and ask God to be present with you and your child as they make decisions affecting their life's work.

Yield. After you've praised, asked, and repented, surrender your child's future to God. While you can advise, counsel, and support your child, only God can guide their spirit. Release your child's decisions, future work, and calling to the Lord, knowing He alone is able to give them perfect direction.

I pray my child will have . . .

    confidence in their abilities
    discovery of talents and gifts
    divine opportunities to use their gifts
    clarity around career choices
    a *strong work ethic* in their career
    wisdom to steward talents well
    a *desire to use spiritual gifts* for others, not for selfish gain
    openness to God's plans
    eagerness to serve the church with their gifts
    creativity and an adventurous spirit
    compassion for others
    discernment of good and evil, right and wrong
    caring mentors, coaches, and leaders
    freedom from perfectionism
    open doors to godly pursuits
    closed doors to unwise opportunities
    a *willingness* to learn and grow
    a *cooperative spirit*
    goals for excellence, not perfection
    connections that create timely opportunities

eagerness to follow God's leading

generosity with resources

courage to follow God's direction

a *willingness* to start small

a healthy *balance* of work and life

godly integrity in the workplace

firmness in the face of criticism or persecution

resolve to follow interests and talents through

financial freedom to explore talents

self-confidence to try new things

resilience to always bounce back

joy when work seems mundane

discernment to know when to say yes or no to opportunities

ingenuity and *industriousness*

perseverance through doubt and fear

readiness to go off the beaten path

an *early discovery* of talents and giftings

complementary giftings to their spouse

giftings protected from corruption

insight regarding financial and career pursuits

Pray through these verses.

I have filled him with the Spirit of God, giving him great wisdom, ability, and expertise in all kinds of crafts.

EXODUS 31:3

I am the LORD your God, who teaches you what is good for you and leads you along the paths you should follow.

ISAIAH 48:17

We know that God causes everything to work together for the good of those who love God and are called according to his purpose for them. For God knew his people in advance, and he chose them to become like his Son, so that his Son would be the firstborn among many brothers and sisters. And having chosen them, he called them to come to him. And having called them, he gave them right standing with himself. And having given them right standing, he gave them his glory.

ROMANS 8:28-30

Sample Prayer —————

God, You chose [child's name] and have given this child Your promised Spirit. May You fill them with wisdom, ability, and expertise in whatever they pursue. Thank You for the gift of this personal guide to enrich their experiences.

_____

_____

_____

_____

_____

_____

_____

_____

_____

_____

_____

_____

You did not choose me, but I chose you. I appointed you to go and produce fruit and that your fruit should remain, so that whatever you ask the Father in my name, he will give you.

JOHN 15:16, CSB

For God's gifts and his call can never be withdrawn.

ROMANS 11:29

Dear brothers and sisters, I plead with you to give your bodies to God because of all he has done for you. Let them be a living and holy sacrifice—the kind he will find acceptable. This is truly the way to worship him.

ROMANS 12:1

Since you are so eager to have the special abilities the Spirit gives, seek those that will strengthen the whole church.

1 CORINTHIANS 14:12

Now these are the gifts Christ gave to the church: the apostles, the prophets, the evangelists, and the pastors and teachers. Their responsibility is to equip God's people to do his work and build up the church, the body of Christ. This will continue until we all come to such unity in our faith and knowledge of God's Son that we will be mature in the Lord, measuring up to the full and complete standard of Christ.

Then we will no longer be immature like children. We won't be tossed and blown about by every wind of new teaching. We will not be influenced when people try to trick us with lies so clever they sound like the truth. Instead, we will speak the truth in love, growing in every way more and more like Christ, who is the head of his body, the church. He makes the whole body fit together perfectly. As each part does its own special work, it helps the other parts grow, so that the whole body is healthy and growing and full of love.

EPHESIANS 4:11-16

Do not neglect the spiritual gift you received through the prophecy spoken over you when the elders of the church laid their hands on you.

1 TIMOTHY 4:14

God has given each of you a gift from his great variety of spiritual gifts. Use them well to serve one another.

1 PETER 4:10

Personalize these prayers.

Opportunity to use gifts.

> I pray, Lord Jesus, You give [child's name] opportunities to use their gifts in natural and age-appropriate ways. May their gifts build up and bless others and point to Your glory! Amen.

Use spiritual gifts for others, not self.

> Lord Jesus, please help [child's name] use their spiritual gifts for Your glory, not so they can boast or outdo others. Please keep their heart humble and turned toward You, and may they recognize that everything good comes from Your hands. Please protect them from pride and selfish ambition. In Jesus' name, amen.

Openness to God's plans.

> Dear Lord, may [child's name] be open to Your plans, Your leading, and Your direction throughout their life. I pray that before acting rashly, making big decisions, or changing course, my child will seek Your will, be obedient to Your Word, and make wise choices. Amen.

Creativity and an adventurous spirit.

God, please help [child's name] be secure in their gifts, calling, and career. Give them a creative and adventurous spirit. Please protect my child from being paralyzed by overthinking or trying to achieve perfection. Help them trust You and not be burdened with decision fatigue. In Jesus' name, amen.

Strong work ethic for career.

I pray [child's name] would take their responsibilities and duties seriously, working hard to finish them and glorify You. Protect my child from being a workaholic. Help them find their life purpose in You, not in a job. May they achieve excellence in everything they do. In Jesus' name, amen.

Lord, be Thou my constant Guide.
Lead me all the way.
Till I reach Thy home at last.
Nevermore to stray. Amen.

LITTLE FOLDED HANDS

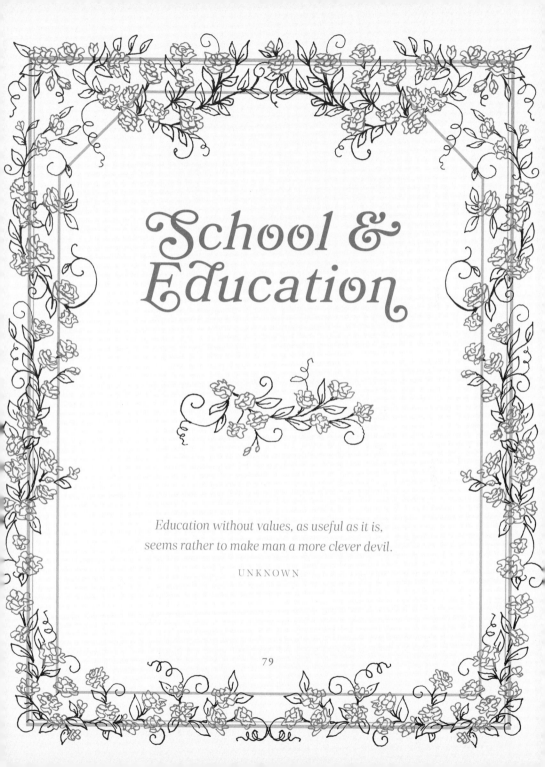

School & Education

*Education without values, as useful as it is,
seems rather to make man a more clever devil.*

UNKNOWN

Our children's education is one of the first big decisions we make regarding their future. Before school age, our little ones are nestled safely with us, influenced by only those we allow into their circles.

Then, suddenly, it's time to start school. Do we homeschool, send our child to a public or a private school, or opt for hybrid schooling? There are several available options, and parents want to make the best choice for their children. This aspect of a child's life takes up a significant amount of their time and is so influential in the molding of their character that it must be done with great thought and prayer.

Praise. Praise God there is so much in this world to learn about. He has made fascinating and creative things that can hold our child's interest and reflect His majesty. Thank God for all the opportunities and options your child has to learn, grow, and cultivate wisdom in their hearts about the natural world around them and the excellence of His ways.

Repent. Ask the Lord to reveal any of your fears, worries, or actions that may have hindered or are currently hindering your child's learning and education. Has God told you to do something you've completely avoided? Do you feel convicted about a certain area of your child's school or education and haven't followed through? Now's the time to discuss it with the Lord.

Ask. Confidently bring your requests before the Lord. Using the prayer prompts as starting points, pour your heart out to God about your dreams for your child. Remind God of His promises and His will; then let the Holy Spirit lead you in the words to pray.

Yield. After you've praised God, brought any lingering issues to Him, and made your requests, release your child's education and schooling to the Lord. Give this important part of your child's life to Him in faith and be assured He will make clear which way to go.

Lord, I pray my child will have . . .

curiosity for learning

passion to dive deeply into subjects

an *understanding* of the importance of education

open doors to the right schools

determination to do the hard work

wisdom with knowledge

caring and insightful *teachers*

strong *critical thinking skills*

ease at absorbing information

freedom from perfectionism

willingness to try new things

a strong *grasp of apologetics*

perseverance through academic challenges

mastery of important subjects

integrity in schoolwork

self-motivation

a rock-solid *biblical worldview*

like-minded school *friends*

a *cooperative attitude*

self-confidence in skills

boldness to speak up

protection from bullying or ostracism

true *comprehension* of important concepts

good behavior and minimal disruptions

success in educational pursuits

courage in the face of adversity

encouraging and *patient teachers*

disciplined *follow-through*

acceptance if a change in the schooling situation *is needed*

a *teacher with godly lesson plans* that reflect Him

an *ability to focus* well

enthusiasm to learn

counsel for handling learning struggles

a *safe school* environment

enriching educational opportunities

good performance under pressure

spiritual clarity that is not deceived by empty doctrines

responsibility to meet deadlines

age-appropriate subjects to study

lessons that integrate spirituality into learning

Pray through these verses.

Give instruction to a wise man, and he
  will be still wiser;
   teach a righteous man, and he will
   . increase in learning.

PROVERBS 9:9, ESV

Teach them to your children. Talk
about them when you are at home
and when you are on the road,
when you are going to bed and
when you are getting up.

DEUTERONOMY 11:19

I believe in your commands;
  now teach me good judgment and
   knowledge.

PSALM 119:66

Let the wise listen to these proverbs
  and become even wiser.
  Let those with understanding
   receive guidance.

PROVERBS 1:5

Intelligent people are always ready to
  learn.
  Their ears are open for knowledge.

PROVERBS 18:15

Sample Prayer —————————

*God, I pray that [child's name] will
be wise and grow wiser with time
and that throughout their life, they
will grow in wisdom and knowledge.*

_____

_____

_____

_____

_____

_____

_____

_____

_____

_____

_____

_____

_____

_____

The fear of the LORD is the beginning
    of knowledge;
  fools despise wisdom and
    instruction.

PROVERBS 1:7, ESV

Wisdom and money can get you almost
    anything,
  but only wisdom can save your life.

ECCLESIASTES 7:12

All your children shall be taught
by the LORD, and great shall be the
peace of your children.

ISAIAH 54:13, ESV

Don't let anyone capture you with
empty philosophies and high-
sounding nonsense that come
from human thinking and from
the spiritual powers of this world,
rather than from Christ.

COLOSSIANS 2:8

If you need wisdom, ask our
generous God, and he will give
it to you. He will not rebuke you
for asking.

JAMES 1:5

Personalize these prayers.

Performs well under pressure.

> Lord Jesus, may [child's name] be able to handle the highs and lows of school. Please equip them with perseverance and grit to keep trying even when things get tough. Give my child endurance, Lord. Amen.

Curiosity for learning.

> God, please give [child's name] a curiosity and a love for learning new things. May You bless them with a teachable heart that will help them gain wisdom, knowledge, and understanding to use throughout their lives. Amen.

Strong critical-thinking skills.

> I pray, Lord Jesus, that You will give [child's name] a sanctified mind. Make them able to think critically and logically so they can face the world without compromising their morals and convictions. Help them not to be swayed by the winds of false doctrines. Amen.

True comprehension of important subjects.

> God, help [child's name] master the basic subjects and
> building blocks of learning so they can succeed in life.
> I pray they would be able to absorb important concepts
> so they can be capable and able to live a godly life that
> blesses others and glorifies You. Amen.

Freedom from perfectionism.

> We know, Lord, that none of us are perfect and that we
> all "fall short of the glory of God" (Romans 3:23, NIV).
> But I pray that You would help spare [child's name] the
> burden and bondage of perfectionism. Instead, please
> help them develop a spirit of excellence that reflects You.
> Amen.

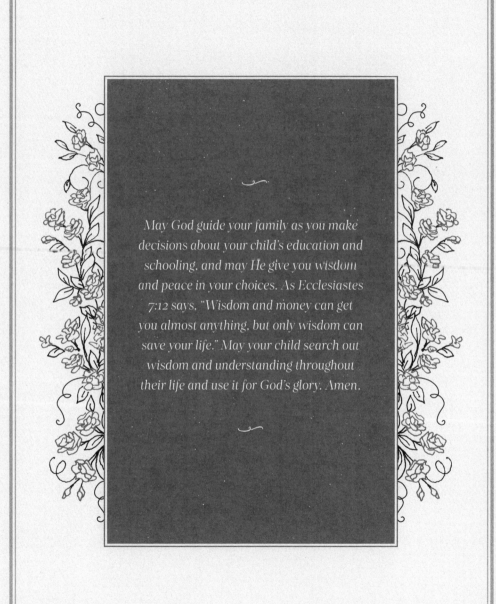

May God guide your family as you make decisions about your child's education and schooling, and may He give you wisdom and peace in your choices. As Ecclesiastes 7:12 says, "Wisdom and money can get you almost anything, but only wisdom can save your life." May your child search out wisdom and understanding throughout their life and use it for God's glory. Amen.

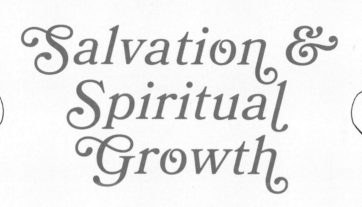

Salvation & Spiritual Growth

Christ is not one of many ways to approach God,
nor is He the best of several ways; He is the only way.

A. W. TOZER

ONE OF OUR DEEPEST DESIRES is for our child's salvation. We want them to know the Lord, to draw near to Him throughout their life, and to follow His will. The world we live in won't lead them to Christ, and we take their salvation seriously within our own homes. It's one of the greatest callings of family life.

Let's jump into how we can pray regarding our child's spiritual journey.

Praise. Choose a prayer prompt and praise God for any positive fruit of spiritual growth in your precious child's life. Thank Him for how you've seen Him draw your child closer or reveal Himself in a special way. Thank God for loving your child, dying for them, and making the narrow path available to your child if they choose to walk it.

Repent. We are human and have fallen short of the glory of God and haven't lived fully for Him. Ask the Lord to reveal where you may have sinned in your spiritual life and take this opportunity to correct your course. Ask God to forgive you if you've set a wrong example for your child, and receive His forgiveness.

Ask. The Scripture commands us to pray and so . . . let us pray. Ask God to carry out His will in the life of your beloved child. Lift up the prayer prompt to Him and share your heart's desire for your child. You don't need to use flowery words; just bring the issue before the Lord.

Yield. Surrender is not for the faint of heart. Be sure you're surrendering the request to God and not to your fears or worries about the future. After you've named the specific topic to the Lord using a prayer prompt, repented where necessary, and asked God to work in your child's life, then place it in God's hands in faith.

Lord, I pray my child shows . . .

humility before God

fear of the Lord

a *recognition and love* for God's presence

evidence of *fruit of the Spirit*

a *readiness to follow* God's will

an *ability to hear God's voice*

a *repentant heart*

enthusiasm to study God's Word

growth in *spiritual gifts*

strong *moral character*

a *heart to share the gospel*

ease in witnessing and sharing their faith

a *teachable heart*

unwavering faith that is steadfast in suffering

delight in serving others

eagerness to memorize Scripture

an *understanding of scriptural principles*

an *awareness of God's hand* in situations

an *aversion to pride*

no compromise with evil

conviction in God's promises

evidence of God's protection from doubt and unbelief

a *love for fellowship* with other believers

a *worshipful, joyful heart*

perseverance in times of questioning
toughness to fight temptations
an understanding of and *protection from deception*
spiritual insight, not spiritual blindness
childlike faith
compassion for others
a *confident attitude* that is not legalistic but doesn't give
    license to sin
the gift of *discernment*
wisdom from the Lord
a deep, abiding *faith in action*
what speaking *truth in love* sounds like
God's power to defeat demonic attack
spiritual brokenness that leads to repentance
integrity in all aspects of life
an *eternal mindset*
God's way to make crooked paths straight
the *evidence of God's intervention*
effective words to defend their faith
a *servant's heart*
conviction and *repentance over sin*
gratitude for spiritual mentors
commitment to carry out God's commands

Pray through these verses.

Joyful are people of integrity,
    who follow the instructions of
        the LORD.
Joyful are those who obey his laws
    and search for him with all their
        hearts.
They do not compromise with evil,
    and they walk only in his paths.

PSALM 119:1-3

Create in me a clean heart, O God.
    Renew a loyal spirit within me.

PSALM 51:10

Those who live in the shelter of the
        Most High
    will find rest in the shadow of the
        Almighty.
This I declare about the LORD:
He alone is my refuge, my place of
        safety;
    he is my God, and I trust him.
For he will rescue you from every trap
    and protect you from deadly
        disease.

Sample Prayer ——————

*Lord God, I pray that [child's name]
would be a person of integrity who
follows Your Word. May [name]
know Your laws by heart, resist evil,
and walk in the paths You've laid
out for their life.*

_____

_____

_____

_____

_____

_____

_____

_____

_____

_____

_____

_____

He will cover you with his feathers.
  He will shelter you with his wings.
  His faithful promises are your
    armor and protection.
Do not be afraid of the terrors of the
    night,
  nor the arrow that flies in the day.
Do not dread the disease that stalks
    in darkness,
  nor the disaster that strikes at
    midday.
Though a thousand fall at your side,
  though ten thousand are dying
    around you,
  these evils will not touch you.

PSALM 91:1-7

Yes, I am the gate. Those who
come in through me will be saved.
They will come and go freely
and will find good pastures. The
thief's purpose is to steal and kill
and destroy. My purpose is to give
them a rich and satisfying life.

JOHN 10:9-10

My sheep listen to my voice; I
know them, and they follow me.
I give them eternal life, and they
will never perish. No one can
snatch them away from me, for
my Father has given them to me,
and he is more powerful than
anyone else. No one can snatch
them from the Father's hand.

JOHN 10:27-29

Yes, I am the vine; you are the
branches. Those who remain in
me, and I in them, will produce
much fruit. For apart from me
you can do nothing.

JOHN 15:5

Don't you see how wonderfully
kind, tolerant, and patient God is
with you? Does this mean nothing
to you? Can't you see that his
kindness is intended to turn you
from your sin?

ROMANS 2:4

You have been called to live in freedom, my brothers and sisters. But don't use your freedom to satisfy your sinful nature. Instead, use your freedom to serve one another in love.

GALATIANS 5:13

Let the message about Christ, in all its richness, fill your lives. Teach and counsel each other with all the wisdom he gives. Sing psalms and hymns and spiritual songs to God with thankful hearts.

COLOSSIANS 3:16

Look! I stand at the door and knock. If you hear my voice and open the door, I will come in, and we will share a meal together as friends.

REVELATION 3:20

Personalize these prayers.

Repentant heart.

Lord, I pray that [child's name] would know when they
have fallen short of Your glory (see Romans 3:23) and
truly believe they are in the wrong. I pray my child
doesn't believe what modern culture says—that they
are perfect no matter what they do. May their heart
be convicted by the truth that they are in desperate
need of a Savior. Keep them coming back to this truth
throughout their life.

God would make crooked paths straight.

Dear Jesus, I lift up [child's name] to You and pray that
You would straighten out the crooked areas in their life
and draw near to them. Convict them whenever they
are living outside of Your will, following sinful desires,
worshiping things rather than You, or allowing their
faith to become lukewarm.

Removal of spiritual blindness.

Please, Lord, open [child's name]'s eyes to see the spiritual support they have in heavenly places. As God opened the eyes of Elisha's servant to see an entire army at the ready (see 2 Kings 6:15-16), may You show my beloved child that You and Your ministering angels are ever present in their life. Be a constant source of strength and encouragement for them.

Love for God's Word.

Lord, please give [child's name] a love for Your Word. Make your Word come alive to them as they open, study, and meditate on Scripture. Let it be more powerful to them than any self-help book or inspiring quote. Make it the plumb line for their life.

Gift of discernment.

I pray [child's name] will have the gift of discernment to guide them throughout their life. Help them recognize which friends, jobs, situations, opportunities, and callings are beneficial, edifying, and from You. Give them wisdom to see and avoid the distractions, dangers, and deceptions that will inevitably come their way.

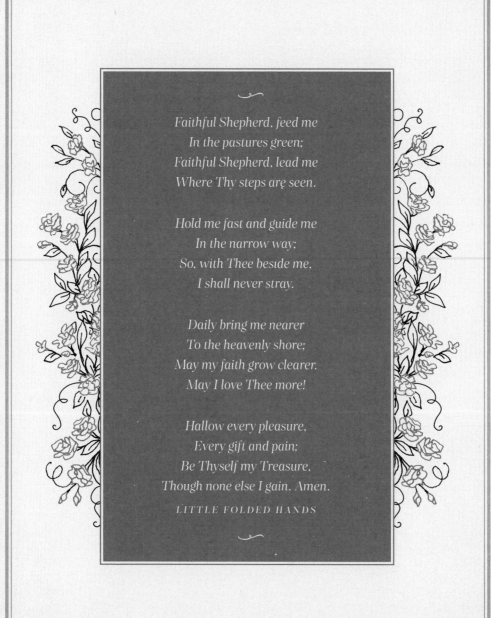

Faithful Shepherd, feed me
In the pastures green;
Faithful Shepherd, lead me
Where Thy steps are seen.

Hold me fast and guide me
In the narrow way;
So, with Thee beside me,
I shall never stray.

Daily bring me nearer
To the heavenly shore;
May my faith grow clearer,
May I love Thee more!

Hallow every pleasure,
Every gift and pain;
Be Thyself my Treasure,
Though none else I gain. Amen.

LITTLE FOLDED HANDS

Friendships

Friendship . . . is born at the moment when one man says to another
"What! You too? I thought that no one but myself . . ."

C. S. LEWIS

Tᴿᵁᴱ ʟɪꜰᴇ-ɢɪᴠɪɴɢ ꜰʀɪᴇɴᴅꜱʜɪᴘꜱ can bring so much joy and comfort to a person. There is camaraderie in the fun times, a shoulder to cry on in the hard times, and everything in between. And the great part about friends is that while you may have a lot of them, one or two faithful friends is usually enough.

Let's pray for your dear child's current and future friendships. Ask God to intervene and send them the right kind of friends at the right time.

Praise. Choose a prayer prompt. Praise and thank God for how you've already seen Him work in your child's life. Thank Him that it's His will we have godly friends, companions, and counsel. Remind God of His words and thank Him that He cares. Praise Him for the godly friends in your life.

Repent. First, be honest with yourself and the Lord. Do you need to repent of, forgive, or release anything that could be holding you back related to this prompt? Is God bringing to mind any issue that needs to be addressed in your own life or in your child's? He will give you wisdom, healing, and direction as you intercede for your child.

Ask. Ask God to grant your heart's desire for your cherished child regarding their friendships. Remind God of His own words and pray those over your child. The Lord knows what you desire and what you fear—candidly confess those things to Him.

Yield. After you've praised, repented, and asked, surrender everything to the Lord to be accomplished in His timing regarding your child's current and future friendships. Empty your heart and mind before God and then release everything into His hands. Keep praying until you feel you've exhausted all you have to say.

Lord, I pray my child will have . . .

true and *deep friendships*
magnetism to attract *godly friends*
healthy *conflict resolution*
timely friendships at various life stages
lifelong friends
protection from bad influences
a *desire to uplift others*
a *willingness to stand up* for friends
loyalty in friendships
an *eagerness* for wise counsel
appropriate boundaries with friends about sin
friends who are *like family*
steadfast, not wishy-washy *affection*
strength in lonely seasons when friends are few
a *firm character* when faced with peer pressure
conviction in their own *identity*
integrity as a friend
a *quick response* to speak well of others
identity in God, not their group of friends
discernment to end unhealthy friendships
fortitude to defend their beliefs
a *close friend* with shared interests
edifying friends
iron-sharpening-iron friends

sense to resist sinful acts with friends

no interest in or attraction to *unhealthy groups*

keenness to recognize true friends

peace when being left out

leadership abilities with their friends

vulnerability to share feelings and struggles

adaptability to be alone, but not become a loner

a *godly shield* against envy and jealousy

intuitive knowledge of when and how to end friendships

deep friendship *bonds with siblings*

a *solid foundation* for parental friendships later

no desire to dominate or control friends

a *propensity to quickly apologize* and make amends

an *awareness* to not be at the wrong places at the wrong
    times

ease in making friends

a *higher value of family* over peer relationships

security against bullying

wisdom to know who is or isn't trustworthy

an *appreciation* for the value of godly friends

a *knack to make friends* of all ages

valuable mentors and counselors

friends who will not hesitate to *lovingly confront* them
    when necessary

Pray through these verses.

There are "friends" who destroy each
other,
but a real friend sticks closer than
a brother.

PROVERBS 18:24

Walk with the wise and become wise;
associate with fools and get in
trouble.

PROVERBS 13:20

The heartfelt counsel of a friend
is as sweet as perfume and incense.
Never abandon a friend—
either yours or your father's.
When disaster strikes, you won't have to
ask your brother for assistance.
It's better to go to a neighbor than
to a brother who lives far away.

PROVERBS 27:9-10

Two people are better off than
one, for they can help each other
succeed. If one person falls, the
other can reach out and help. But
someone who falls alone is in real
trouble.

ECCLESIASTES 4:9-10

Sample Prayer ————

*God, I pray that [child's name]
would have a true and deep
friendship with a fellow believer
who will help [name] focus on you,
offer encouragement throughout
their life, and teach them what it's
like to stick with someone who sticks
with You in times of great need.*

_____

_____

_____

_____

_____

_____

_____

_____

_____

_____

_____

_____

Do to others as you would like them to do to you.

LUKE 6:31

❧

This is my commandment: Love each other in the same way I have loved you. There is no greater love than to lay down one's life for one's friends.

JOHN 15:12-13

❧

Love each other with genuine affection, and take delight in honoring each other.

ROMANS 12:10

❧

Don't be fooled by those who say such things, for "bad company corrupts good character."

1 CORINTHIANS 15:33

❧

Share each other's burdens, and in this way obey the law of Christ.

GALATIANS 6:2

❧

Encourage each other and build each other up, just as you are already doing.

1 THESSALONIANS 5:11

Personalize these prayers.

Willingness to stand up for friends.

> Lord God, I pray [child's name] will be brave and
> willing to stand up to anyone who gossips, mistreats,
> or otherwise harms their friends. May [name] have
> strong convictions and become a true support to their
> close friends, and may these friends be there for them
> in return.

Loyalty in friendships.

> Dear Jesus, may [child's name] find friends who
> are loyal and steadfast, not wishy-washy with their
> affection or friendship. Please protect my child
> from fair-weather friends, Lord, and lead them into
> life-giving friendships.

Attracts godly friends.

> God, I pray [child's name] would be able to find godly
> friends with whom they share interests, hobbies, and
> activities. Please put people in my child's life who will
> help keep them on the narrow road and point them
> to Christ their entire life.

Strength in lonely seasons.

Lord Jesus, we know everyone goes through periods of loneliness in their life. For children, it often revolves around changes they have no control over—leaving friends and what is familiar and moving to new places with new schools. I pray that [child's name] would turn to You in their seasons of loneliness. Comfort their heart and bring them the right friends at the right time.

Identity in God, not their peer group.

Lord God, may [child's name] be secure in their own identity, personality, and interests. I pray they would be able to be their own person and not change depending on who their friends are. God, please help them to be comfortable in their own skin and send friends their way whom they can be authentic with.

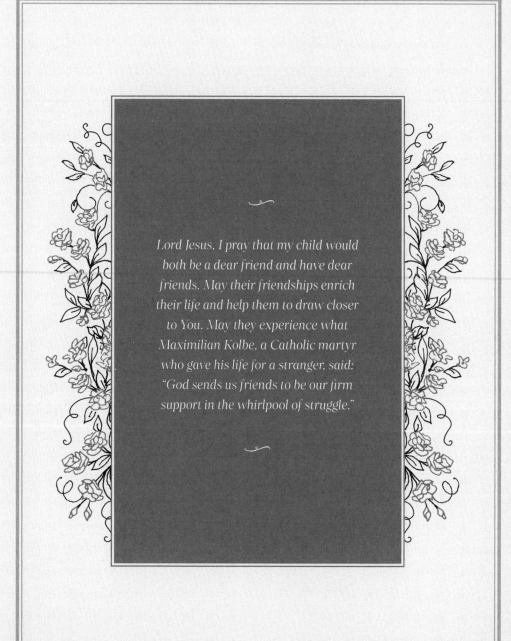

Lord Jesus, I pray that my child would both be a dear friend and have dear friends. May their friendships enrich their life and help them to draw closer to You. May they experience what Maximilian Kolbe, a Catholic martyr who gave his life for a stranger, said: "God sends us friends to be our firm support in the whirlpool of struggle."

Love & Marriage

If I had a flower for every time I thought of you . . .
I could walk through my garden forever.

ATTRIBUTED TO ALFRED, LORD TENNYSON

It's been said many times in many ways that who we marry sets the course for our lives. To some extent, it can determine our happiness and our life's direction. Because of this, it's important for us to think of this significant step for our precious child. We always want the best for them, and we want them to marry well.

And by *well*, we mean someone with good character, a love for Jesus, a kind heart, and wisdom to make good choices. That's quite a tall order! As we pray over our child's maturing love and the possibility of a future married life, let's lift our hearts up to the living God who knows exactly what we need even before we utter it.

Praise. Let's praise God that He knows our precious child's heart and their needs and desires more than we ever could. He created them, and He has an excellent plan for them. We can thank Him for loving our child, regardless of whether they ever marry or find love. God's unfailing love is more than enough to fill and satisfy every person's heart. Choose a prayer prompt and then praise or thank God for anything you think of related to the topic.

Repent. If there's some way you have fallen short in your own marriage, confess and ask God to show you what steps you need to take. God will help you make the changes necessary. Depending on your child's age, do they need counsel in this area? Be candid with your child and ask God to convict them. Pray that you can have honest and productive discussions with your child about love and relationships.

Ask. Using a prayer prompt, lift up your child's current (or future) romance or love life to the Lord. Ask the Lord to make any crooked paths straight and for Him to help your child choose a godly spouse. Or, if it's His will for them to remain single, ask that they will be content and pure and find great purpose in their singleness.

Yield. I don't know about you, but there are days when I'm annoyed that I don't control the universe. But more often, I'm extremely thankful I don't have that responsibility. It is hard when so much of our precious child's life is outside of our control, isn't it? But praise God, He is in control! Pray through the prompts that speak to you and then surrender them to God. Bear the burden momentarily in prayer; then release the burden to your Savior.

Lord, I pray that if marriage is part of Your plan for my child, they will have . . .

> *wisdom* in the choice of a spouse
> *equal yoking*
> *recognition of red flags* when dating
> a *healthy communication* style
> *acceptance* of whatever life season they are in
> *peace*, not desperation in seeking a spouse
> *sexual purity* before and during marriage
> *faithfulness* in their relationship
> *honor and respect* for the person they love
> *protection* from sexual confusion
> *compatible callings*
> a *complementary personality* with their partner
> *humility and discernment* to choose a humble person
> a commitment to *integrity*
> a *longing* to find someone who also seeks God
> an *ability to hear God*'s direction
> a *partner* who is *free of addiction*
> *protection from abuse* and mistreatment
> a *genuine love* for their spouse
> an *encouraging heart* to build the other person up
> *prayerful* and united *decision-making*
> a *harmonious family*
> clear and *responsible actions*
> *sensitivity to God's plan* for the family
> *healthy dating* habits

an *awareness and attraction* to a godly person
safety in relationship
an ability to start *a family*
examples of healthy patterns of living
biblical standards for their relationship
joy and gratitude for family members
strength to endure adversity together
a *healthy balance* of work and family
a *peaceful home* environment
a *sense of purpose* in family life
a *desire to reflect God's love* as a parent
godly conflict resolution
oneness in family goals
satisfaction with the spouse of their youth
clear direction on their choice of a spouse
life-giving relationships with in-laws
no issue prioritizing their spouse over friends
quick responses to solve relationship problems
an *iron-sharpening-iron mindset*
a deep *abiding friendship*
a *commitment to honesty* and integrity
godly mentors and wise counsel
strength to handle stress that threatens to divide
loyalty and unity even in conflict
shared interests and hobbies

Pray through these verses.

Don't team up with those who are unbelievers. How can righteousness be a partner with wickedness? How can light live with darkness?

2 CORINTHIANS 6:14

Love and faithfulness meet together;
    righteousness and peace kiss
        each other.
Faithfulness springs forth from
        the earth,
    and righteousness looks down
        from heaven.

PSALM 85:10-11, NIV

Houses and wealth are inherited
        from parents,
    but a prudent wife is from
        the LORD.

PROVERBS 19:14, NIV

Two people are better off than one, for they can help each other succeed. If one person falls, the other can reach out and help. But someone who falls alone is in real trouble.

ECCLESIASTES 4:9-10

Sample Prayer ——————

Jesus, may [child's name] be patient and kind in their romantic relationships. May [name] display Christlike love before and during marriage, being generous and honoring their partner.

————————————

————————————

————————————

————————————

————————————

————————————

————————————

————————————

————————————

————————————

————————————

————————————

I found my love!

SONG OF SONGS 5:4

❧

Be completely humble and gentle;
be patient, bearing with one
another in love.

EPHESIANS 4:2, NIV

❧

Over all these virtues put on love,
which binds them all together
in perfect unity. Let the peace of
Christ rule in your hearts, since
as members of one body you were
called to peace. And be thankful.

COLOSSIANS 3:14-15, NIV

❧

Give honor to marriage, and
remain faithful to one another
in marriage.

HEBREWS 13:4

Personalize these prayers.

Discernment to identify red flags in dating.

> Lord, I pray [child's name] will walk with the Holy
> Spirit throughout their life and especially when
> considering a spouse. May they be able to recognize the
> true character of the person they love and be able to
> act wisely as they pursue a relationship that honors You
> and Your plan for their life.

Faithfulness in relationship.

> May You help [child's name] be an honest, faithful, and
> caring spouse. I pray they value commitment, integrity,
> and the type of love You lay out in 1 Corinthians 13
> so the marriage will be a source of joy and strength
> throughout their life.

Humility in both partners.

> Lord God, I pray [child's name] and their future
> spouse will keep "short accounts" with each other and
> quickly discuss any issues or struggles with humility
> and a spirit of cooperation. May their challenges make
> their commitment even stronger and bring them closer
> together.

Unity in family goals.

As [child's name] and their spouse do life together, I
pray they will be wise about their life direction and
the decisions they make, regularly praying and seeking
Your will for their lives. May they be focused and alert,
listening to where You would have them go and what
You would have them do.

Iron sharpening iron.

Lord, I pray Proverbs 27:17 would be true in [child's
name]'s marriage. "As iron sharpens iron," may my child's
spouse help refine them, challenge them in their faith
and character, bring them closer to You, and help them
to become more like You throughout their life.

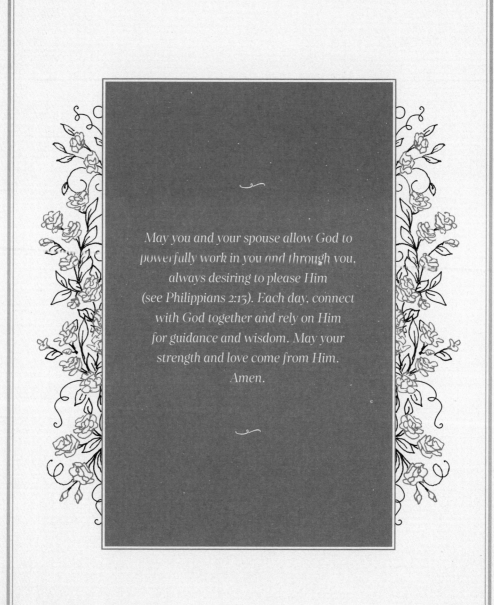

May you and your spouse allow God to powerfully work in you and through you, always desiring to please Him (see Philippians 2:15). Each day, connect with God together and rely on Him for guidance and wisdom. May your strength and love come from Him. Amen.

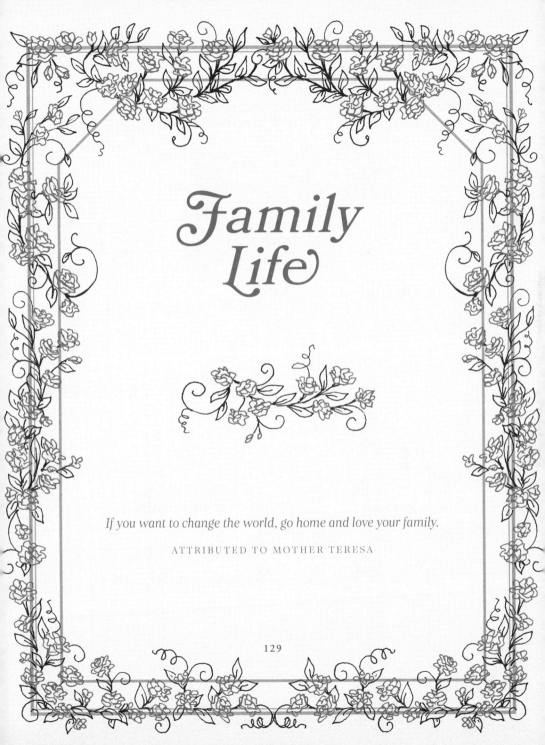

Family Life

If you want to change the world, go home and love your family.

ATTRIBUTED TO MOTHER TERESA

CHILDREN ARE A BLESSING from the Lord. Their purehearted love and loyalty pull on a mother's heartstrings like nothing else does. Most of us want nothing more than to raise our precious children in a happy and peaceful home.

Then life happens. There are trials, troubles, and seasons of stress for a family. But even during these times, we can find deep peace with God as we parent in a way that honors Him and demonstrates His love to our children.

Praise. Picture your family in your mind and think about each individual person, as well as all of you together. Lift up your praise to the Lord for your family—out loud in prayer or song or written down in a journal. Were there any trials or obstacles to family life that the Lord removed? Were there answers to prayer you want to thank God for? Thank and praise Him for your child, for knitting them together in your womb, and for keeping His eyes on them throughout their entire life.

Repent. With a humble and teachable heart, ask the Lord to reveal anything that needs to be repented of or changed in your family. Are there areas of responsibility where you've departed from your convictions? Has the Lord asked you to do something for your family that hasn't been done yet? Evaluate and recalibrate your heart, knowing that the Lord deals graciously with those who repent.

Ask. Let any feelings, hopes, or regrets you have about your family's dynamics surface as you sit with the Lord and ready your heart in prayer. We can come boldly to the throne of God (see Hebrews 4:16), so take time to make your requests known to Him. Confidently bring your heartfelt appeals to the Lord. Are there things your family desperately needs right now? Do you need God to show up in situations that are beyond your ability to effect change? Do you have hopes and dreams for the future that line up with God's will? Take some time to bring these up in prayer, using the list of prompts for inspiration.

Yield. After you've prayed through your specific requests, surrender them to God. Prayer builds our faith, and surrendering our hearts' deepest desires to God builds our trust. Nothing is gained by worrying, but peace is gained by release.

℘ pray each family member experiences . . .

a *loving home* atmosphere
healthy *conflict resolutions*
long-lasting *sibling relationships*
genuine affection for one another
short accounts for disagreements
godly behavior toward one another
protection against grudges and hard feelings
a *willingness to forgive* one another
lots of *fun memories* together
healthy boundaries with family members
no favoritism or cliquish behavior
space and courtesy when they need quiet
respect and kindness from everyone
protection against abuse or bullying
togetherness and loyalty
listening ears and empathizing hearts
examples of respect for authority
friendly, not destructive, *competition*
feelings of *safety at home*
open and *honest communication*
comfort during difficult talks
servant-heartedness toward one another

a *peaceful pace* of family life
a *voice in* family *scheduling*
a *cooperative team spirit* in regard to chores
wisdom and experienced *counsel* to make good choices
more time together than apart
health and safety as a family
enough *resources* to meet needs
an *abiding faith* as a family
gracious attitudes during trials
protection against bitterness and resentment
an *understanding of* the overall *family vision*
God's discerning light to illuminate secrets
a vibrant *church community* for worship
family *opportunities to serve*
a *legacy of Christ followers* for generations
healthy and *encouraging parental authority*
conviction when family life has gone awry
evidence of *God's faithfulness*
ease in talking about spiritual things
firm boundaries in place against sinful behaviors
wholesome actions and interests
generational *curses being broken*

Pray through these verses.

I could have no greater joy than to hear that my children are following the truth.

3 JOHN 1:4

Your descendants will be as numerous as the dust of the earth! They will spread out in all directions—to the west and the east, to the north and the south. And all the families of the earth will be blessed through you and your descendants.

GENESIS 28:14

You must commit yourselves wholeheartedly to these commands that I am giving you today. Repeat them again and again to your children. Talk about them when you are at home and when you are on the road, when you are going to bed and when you are getting up.

DEUTERONOMY 6:6-7

Sample Prayer —————

Lord Jesus, I pray You draw [child's name] to You throughout their entire life. I lift my child up to You and pray they would become a true and dedicated follower of Christ.

_____

_____

_____

_____

_____

_____

_____

_____

_____

_____

_____

_____

_____

The love of the LORD remains forever
　　with those who fear him.
His salvation extends to the children's
　　children
　　　of those who are faithful to his
　　　covenant,
　　　of those who obey his
　　　commandments!

PSALM 103:17-18

Children are a gift from the LORD;
　　they are a reward from him.
Children born to a young man
　　are like arrows in a warrior's
　　hands.
How joyful is the man whose quiver
　　is full of them!

PSALM 127:3-5

How wonderful and pleasant it is
　　when brothers live together in
　　harmony!

PSALM 133:1

Grandchildren are the crowning glory
　　of the aged;
　　parents are the pride of their
　　children.

PROVERBS 17:6

Jesus called for the children and said to the disciples, "Let the children come to me. Don't stop them! For the Kingdom of God belongs to those who are like these children."

LUKE 18:16

"Believe in the Lord Jesus, and you will be saved, you and your household." And they spoke the word of the Lord to him and to all who were in his house. And he took them the same hour of the night and washed their wounds; and he was baptized at once, he and all his family. Then he brought them up into his house and set food before them. And he rejoiced along with his entire household that he had believed in God.

ACTS 16:31-34, ESV

Bear with each other and forgive one another if any of you has a grievance against someone. Forgive as the Lord forgave you.

COLOSSIANS 3:13, NIV

Personalize these prayers.

Loving family and home atmosphere.

> Lord, I pray that our home atmosphere would be filled with peace and calm, not stress. Even if conflicts arise, we are in hectic seasons, or have difficult circumstances, please help us to continually make choices that will allow harmony and safety to reign in our home.

Protection against grudges and hard feelings.

> Dear Jesus, we know that when we live with other people, misunderstandings and hurt feelings can happen. I pray that we'd never brush situations under the rug or permit bitter roots of unforgiveness to linger among family members. Please help us to resolve issues quickly so resentment doesn't fester. In Jesus' name, amen.

No favoritism or cliquish behavior.

> God, please help everyone to deeply feel a part of this family. I know there will be shared interests among some and not others, or seasons where certain siblings get along better than others, but I pray that no child or adult in the family will ever feel left out or less than anyone else.

Protection against abuse or bullying.

Lord God, I pray against any type of evil, abuse, bullying, or mistreatment of one family member by another. Please, God, may we pay close attention to the Holy Spirit's leading and make sure nobody is perpetrating any abuse within our own walls.

Ability to listen and empathize.

God, I pray our home would be the place where each family member feels heard and understood. Help me to sense and see when emotions are high or my child has an unspoken need. In those instances, speak through me and help me to emotionally support my child in godly ways. In Jesus' name, amen.

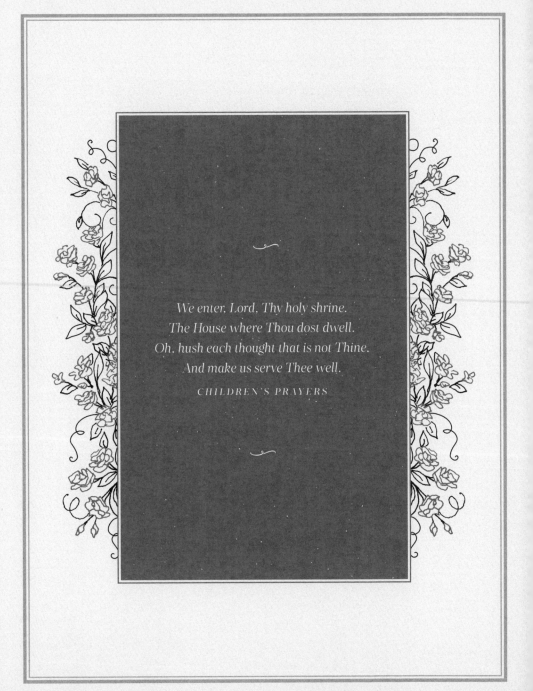

We enter, Lord, Thy holy shrine,
The House where Thou dost dwell,
Oh, hush each thought that is not Thine,
And make us serve Thee well.

CHILDREN'S PRAYERS

Finances

All that is gold does not glitter.

J. R. R. TOLKIEN

MONEY IS MENTIONED more than two thousand times in the Bible, even more than faith or prayer! Obviously, it's a topic to take seriously. Whether your child is old enough to even know what money is or not, there's no time like the present to begin building a godly foundation for their future financial success through prayer.

Praise. Choose a prayer prompt for your precious child today. Praise God for how He has acted in your own finances or perhaps already in your child's finances. Thank Him for His provision and providence. Open your heart to God to receive His instruction as you petition the Lord on behalf of your child.

Repent. If you are personally convicted about the topic of money, praise God! Repent and ask the Lord for wisdom to help you change course. Has your family made bad financial decisions that have cost you? There's no time like the present to reorient and realign your own attitudes and mindset with that of Scripture. Ask God to show you if there's anything in the area of finances that needs to be addressed.

Ask. James 4:2 says, "You don't have what you want because you don't ask God for it." With your prayer prompt in mind, ask the Lord to hear and answer your request. Read Scripture that applies to money, repeat God's own words, and understand His heart on this matter. Let the Holy Spirit lead you as you pray and be willing to sit with your request as long as needed.

Yield. After you've prayed it through, release it to God. While we are in control of many financial decisions in our lives, we aren't in control of the circumstances outside of us and our precious children. Believe that God is the one in control and we can only bring our requests to Him, trusting He has heard us.

Lord, I pray my child develops . . .

diligence in tithing

joyful tithing, not obligatory giving

generosity with resources

freedom from money worries

hope not centered in wealth

responsible *saving practices*

wisdom with investments

avoidance of crippling debt

thoughtful vs. compulsive *spending* habits

protection from greed or love of money

compounding wealth

an *industrious mindset*

a *strong work ethic*

an *ability to delay gratification*

favorable *financial opportunities*

a *judicious sense of timing* in finances

an *understanding of* basic *economics*

protection from materialism

honest financial *gains*

a *cautious awareness* against get-rich-quick schemes

a clear *sense of career options*

thorough financial *planning*

purposeful giving

faith for financial *provision*

pursuits of godly endeavors with money

contentment in finances

an *attitude of appreciation,* not entitlement
a *willingness to seek experienced* financial *advisers*
integrity in money matters
perseverance in times of financial stress
ways to prevent poverty
a *love of eternal things* over money
a fair *solution for financial justice* when wronged
timely responses to job opportunities
insight regarding the financial environment
prosperity
prudence with taxes
accelerated *debt payoff*
opportunities to create income
a *lender's* not a borrower's *mindset*
an *inheritance* for both their children and their children's
    children
a *discreet generosity,* not done for self-importance or for show
a *heart to support God's work*
a *time to enjoy the fruits of labor* with others
good *stewardship*
blessings from the work of their hands *to benefit others*
an unwavering *desire to give* rather than receive
caution against overworking to accumulate wealth
a *heart centered on God,* not money
wealth that doesn't pull them away from God

Pray through these verses.

Give me neither poverty nor
    riches!
Give me just enough to satisfy my
    needs.
For if I grow rich, I may deny you and
    say, "Who is the LORD?"
    And if I am too poor, I may steal
    and thus insult God's holy
    name.

PROVERBS 30:8-9

The LORD will send rain at the
proper time from his rich treasury
in the heavens and will bless all
the work you do. You will lend to
many nations, but you will never
need to borrow from them.

DEUTERONOMY 28:12

All the animals of the forest are mine,
    and I own the cattle on a thousand
    hills.

PSALM 50:10

Honor the LORD with your wealth
    and with the best part of
    everything you produce.

PROVERBS 3:9

Sample Prayer ―――――

*God, please provide the right
amount of financial resources for
[child's name] throughout their
entire life. Make the supply not so
much that [name] relies on that
resource rather than You, and not so
little as to lead them into procuring
money through sinful means or
causing extreme distress. Please show
yourself as [name]'s caring provider!*

Wealth from get-rich-quick schemes
    quickly disappears;
  wealth from hard work grows over
    time.

PROVERBS 13:11

Those who love money will never
have enough. How meaningless
to think that wealth brings true
happiness!

ECCLESIASTES 5:10

Don't store up treasures here on
earth, where moths eat them and
rust destroys them, and where
thieves break in and steal. Store
your treasures in heaven, where
moths and rust cannot destroy,
and thieves do not break in and
steal. Wherever your treasure is,
there the desires of your heart will
also be. . . .

    No one can serve two masters.
For you will hate one and love
the other; you will be devoted to
one and despise the other. You
cannot serve God and be enslaved
to money.

MATTHEW 6:19-21, 24

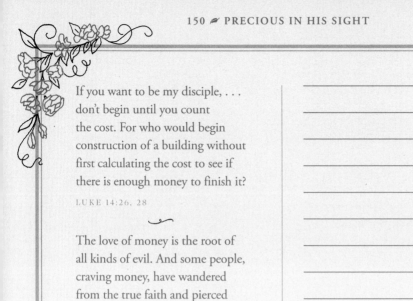

If you want to be my disciple, . . .
don't begin until you count
the cost. For who would begin
construction of a building without
first calculating the cost to see if
there is enough money to finish it?

LUKE 14:26, 28

The love of money is the root of
all kinds of evil. And some people,
craving money, have wandered
from the true faith and pierced
themselves with many sorrows.

1 TIMOTHY 6:10

Don't love money; be satisfied with
what you have. For God has said,

"I will never fail you.
    I will never abandon you."

HEBREWS 13:5

Personalize these prayers.

Hope not centered in wealth.

Lord Jesus, I pray [child's name] would not put their hope, safety, and security in money or the pursuit of wealth but in You. Whether their funds are extremely limited or plentiful, may they know that everything comes from You, not from their own efforts. Give them contentment in every financial circumstance they find themselves in.

Good steward.

Dear God, may [child's name] be a good steward of all the blessings You give them. Whether it's finances and assets or the talents and skills You've given them to earn a living, help them be responsible and wise in how they use these gifts. May their resources bless their lives and the lives of others, and may they not be a stumbling block to godly living.

Protection from materialism.

Lord God, Your Word says we cannot serve two masters—God and money. I pray [child's name] would make You, not money, the center of their life. When they are making important life decisions, help them realize financial matters are not the only determining factors that come into play. May their financial situation draw them closer to You, not further from Your will.

Sense of timing in finances.

God in heaven, I pray [child's name] would have a solid understanding of the financial environment around them, coupled with the season of life they're experiencing. Lord Jesus, may they make wise financial decisions and feel the Holy Spirit's leading when they need to make important judgments regarding money. Let them accurately gauge the economic times, seek counsel if needed, and act prudently and appropriately.

Contentment in finances.

Dear Lord, Your Word says to be content in all circumstances, and I pray [child's name] would feel that contentment no matter what their financial situation is. Whether they are working to improve their finances, trying to get their spending under control, or creating a plan to increase their savings or investments, I pray they will be confident that You will provide all their needs throughout their entire life.

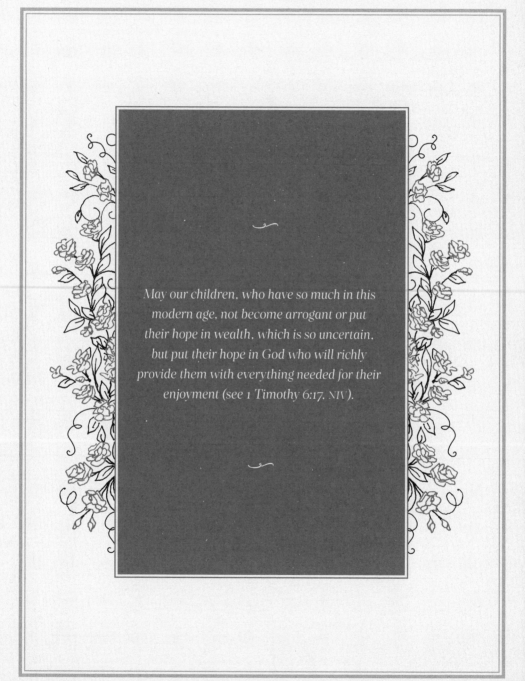

May our children, who have so much in this modern age, not become arrogant or put their hope in wealth, which is so uncertain, but put their hope in God who will richly provide them with everything needed for their enjoyment (see 1 Timothy 6:17, NIV).

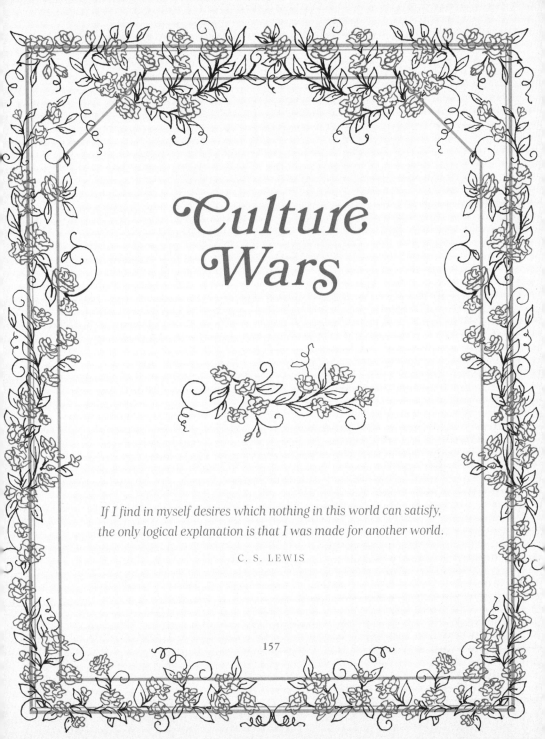

Culture Wars

If I find in myself desires which nothing in this world can satisfy,
the only logical explanation is that I was made for another world.

C. S. LEWIS

WE CANNOT ESCAPE the world we are living in. Our children grow up in families, communities, schools, churches, and social groups with other people from various backgrounds. The people who influence our kids may or may not believe God's Word, and their actions may not be godly. Even so, we are called to be a light to the world, to share God's love with others, and to disciple those who want to follow Jesus.

The difficulty comes with living in the world and not becoming more and more like the world. The allure is real, the temptation is there, and we want to raise our kids to be able to live in the world while being citizens of heaven. It's not an easy task, but we will persevere.

Praise. Praise the Lord for all the beautiful and lovely parts of this world. Sunrises and sunsets, flowers, animals, friends, the ability to work, and anything else that comes to mind. God made everything on earth, and it all reflects His glory. Ask Him to highlight anything you are grateful for.

Repent. Allow the Holy Spirit to convict you in the ways you've allowed the world and its teachings to seep in and corrupt parts of your faith. Have you let doubt set in because you entertained worldly teachings? At some point in your life, did you go off the rails and engage in behaviors that the world said was okay, even though God's Word spoke against them? Be vulnerable and penitent, offering these confessions to God. Ask Him to show you anything that needs to be revealed and accept His forgiveness and grace.

Ask. Pray that the Lord will move mightily in your child's life—protecting them from harm and establishing a firm and godly foundation in their life. Use the prayer prompts to dive into deep intercessory prayer for your child. We know that God hears us when we ask according to His will. Don't hesitate to reveal your heart's desire for your child to Him.

Yield. When you are finished with today's prayer session, release everything to the Lord. Stand in faith, firm in your conviction that God loves your child more than you possibly can. Allow God to move and work according to His timing and plans. When doubt creeps into your mind, bring the issue back to the Lord.

*L*ord, give my child . . .

discernment between good and evil
godly friends, mentors, and family
fervor for evangelism
perseverance to tackle doubt and questioning
spiritual eyes to see the world
a *biblical worldview*
strong biblical *convictions*
protection from falling into besetting sin
resistance to temptations
admission of sin, not hidden sin that has room to grow
freedom from materialism
power to stand up for what's right
peace when they break rank with peers
understanding of Scripture from a young age
comfort with not fitting in
protection from deception
awareness and conviction against twisting Scripture
    to fit culture
endurance during persecution
ready answers for their faith
a *like-minded peer group*
disciplined use and careful searches on devices
a healthy *self-confidence*

no curiosity, interest, or draw *toward the occult*

an *eternal perspective* and mindset

determination to walk in the Spirit, not in the flesh

a *deep thirst* for God's Word

assurance in biblical teachings, not swayed by false
   doctrines

discernment to test words and ideas against Scripture

a *thick skin* for criticism

a *teachable heart* toward God

correct handling of *truth*

wisdom as that of a serpent, harmlessness as of a dove

unswerving trust in God's Word over feelings

victory over doubts and fears

strong resolve to do what's biblically right

a *passion* to do God's will

a *repentant heart* before God

a *belief in what's true*, not what feels right

a *desire to be authentic* and not to perform

release from people-pleasing tendencies

acceptance of God's Word over people's words

healthy and *fertile soil in their heart*

a *foundation* in biblical knowledge

critical thinking skills

Pray through these verses.

Don't copy the behavior and customs of this world, but let God transform you into a new person by changing the way you think. Then you will learn to know God's will for you, which is good and pleasing and perfect.

ROMANS 12:2

The world would love you as one of its own if you belonged to it, but you are no longer part of the world. I chose you to come out of the world, so it hates you.

JOHN 15:19

I'm not asking you to take them out of the world, but to keep them safe from the evil one. They do not belong to this world any more than I do.

JOHN 17:15-16

Sample Prayer

Lord God, I know culture is a strong force and could lead [child's name] away from You. Help them use Your Word as their guide and influence instead of the ever-changing ways of the world.

Do you not know that your body is a temple of the Holy Spirit within you, whom you have from God? You are not your own.

1 CORINTHIANS 6:19, ESV

Don't team up with those who are unbelievers. How can righteousness be a partner with wickedness? How can light live with darkness?

2 CORINTHIANS 6:14

Let the Holy Spirit guide your lives. Then you won't be doing what your sinful nature craves.

GALATIANS 5:16

We are citizens of heaven, where the Lord Jesus Christ lives. And we are eagerly waiting for him to return as our Savior.

PHILIPPIANS 3:20

Put on your new nature, and be renewed as you learn to know your Creator and become like him.

COLOSSIANS 3:10

If you keep yourself pure, you will be a special utensil for honorable use. Your life will be clean, and you will be ready for the Master to use you for every good work.

2 TIMOTHY 2:21

But you are not like that, for you are a chosen people. You are royal priests, a holy nation, God's very own possession. As a result, you can show others the goodness of God, for he called you out of the darkness into his wonderful light.

1 PETER 2:9

Personalize these prayers.

No draw toward the occult.

God, protect [child's name] from being curious and interested in the occult and New Age practices or groups. Please keep their heart focused on You, and let any desire for the supernatural be grounded in Scripture, revealed by Your Spirit, and focused on You and Your will for their life. Let their spiritual journey with You be exciting and adventurous. In Jesus' name, amen.

A godly peer group.

Father God, fortify [child's name]'s biblical teaching by surrounding them with friends and peer groups who value God's Word over cultural norms. Please protect my child from being tossed to and fro, full of doubt and wishy-washiness toward the church and faith in You. Help them establish consistent Scripture-reading practices that keep them aligned with Your truth. Amen.

Strong biblical convictions.

Dear Lord, in the face of a culture that is upside down and backwards, help [child's name] develop and maintain strong biblical convictions. May they never water down their beliefs or give way to temptation but be motivated by Your Spirit to follow Your Word, rather than what culture says is okay. In Jesus' name, amen.

An understanding of Scripture.

God, please help me to regularly expose [child's name] to Your Word and foster in them a deep love for and keen interest in Scripture. Reveal Yourself to them as they read and study Your Word. May they be so familiar with what You say that they will readily discern any false teachings and lies. Amen.

An ability to defend their faith.

Dear Jesus, give [child's name] an unshakable foundation of faith so they always have a ready answer for why they trust You. I pray they will freely share their faith with others and talk about what You have done in their life. In Jesus' name, amen.

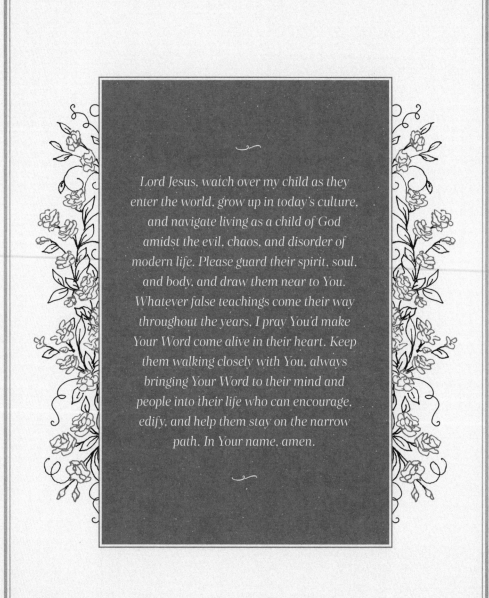

Lord Jesus, watch over my child as they enter the world, grow up in today's culture, and navigate living as a child of God amidst the evil, chaos, and disorder of modern life. Please guard their spirit, soul, and body, and draw them near to You. Whatever false teachings come their way throughout the years, I pray You'd make Your Word come alive in their heart. Keep them walking closely with You, always bringing Your Word to their mind and people into their life who can encourage, edify, and help them stay on the narrow path. In Your name, amen.

I pray that as you intercede for your precious ones, you will grow closer to both your Father in heaven, and your children on earth.

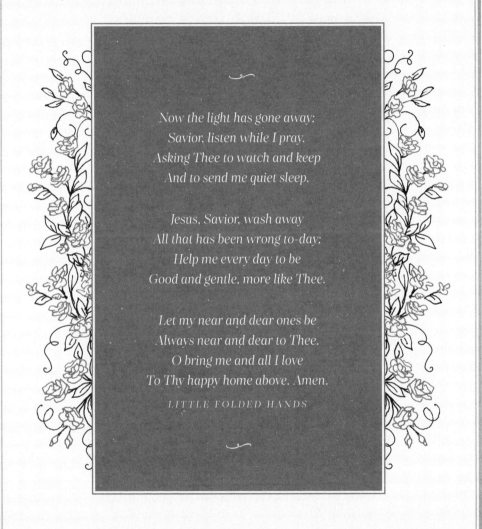

Now the light has gone away;
Savior, listen while I pray.
Asking Thee to watch and keep
And to send me quiet sleep.

Jesus, Savior, wash away
All that has been wrong to-day;
Help me every day to be
Good and gentle, more like Thee.

Let my near and dear ones be
Always near and dear to Thee.
O bring me and all I love
To Thy happy home above. Amen.

LITTLE FOLDED HANDS

About the
Author

⁓

℞achel Norman is a mother, a parenting coach, a certified sleep consultant, and the founder of A Mother Far from Home, an online community dedicated to helping young mothers create peaceful and enjoyable lives for their families. Her website focuses on family and personal routines, boundaries, healthy sleep habits, and emotional and mental well-being for both parents and children.

Before founding A Mother Far from Home in 2012, Rachel earned her bachelor's degree in criminology and law and her master's degree in public administration. Upon graduation, she completed a TESOL (Teachers of English to Speakers of Other Languages) certificate and for a couple of years, lived in Italy, where she became fluent in Italian. She then attended a discipleship program in England, where she met her husband, and they spent the next few years living in Scotland and Australia as they grew their family.

Having five babies in five years gave her a passion for family life, which inspired the creation of her online business. Today, she has more than 100,000 followers on social media and 110,000-plus subscribers to her weekly parenting newsletter. She also continues to encourage more than a million mothers a year on her website.

Rachel resides in DeFuniak Springs, Florida, with her husband, Matthew, and their five young children. She loves the beach, boating, traveling, reading, and being with her family.

Also by

Rachel Norman

*Available everywhere
books are sold.*